The Girls Behind the Guns

With the ATS in World War II

DOROTHY BREWER KERR

ROBERT HALE · LONDON

Photoset in Palatino by
Derek Doyle & Associates, Mold, Clwyd.
Printed in Great Britain by
St Edmundsbury Press, Bury St Edmunds, Suffolk.
Bound by WBC Bookbinders Limited.

Contents

Illustrations

Between pages 64 and 65

PICTURE CREDITS
Numbers 4, 5 and 8 are in Crown Copyright.

1 'Your Country Needs You!'

London, 1940–41

My decision to join the Army, the Auxiliary Territorial Service, was taken in the twinkling of an eye. Between one raindrop and the next, one day in early June 1941, on the bus on the way to work. There had been no air raids on London for three weeks, and the children at school had had a few nights' sleep. It had been ludicrous, trying to take lessons all that spring between one night's bombardment and the next.

The RAF had proved that they could defend us against anything they could see; but at night it was a different matter. Only our anti-aircraft guns stood against the raiders in the darkness, with only the searchlights to help them. They made a lot of encouraging noise, but their hits were few and far between.

I rubbed a place on the bus window, to see through. No use. It was bucketing down. What should I do? On the one hand, carry on at school. Perhaps it was my duty. Teaching was already a reserved occupation for all women over the age of twenty-five, and it was to be reduced to twenty in September. I'd be trapped. But I must complete my year's probation, to confirm my certificate. It was only fair to my parents. August. It would be cutting it fine.

I knew who would come and sit beside me on the bus: Mr Harris, who taught at a school near mine, in Manor Park. He was a kind man, giving me his company and the benefit of his predictable thoughts each morning, for the twenty minutes of the journey. There was one more stop before his. Oh, would nobody else ever sit next to me? What should I do? The WRNS wanted cooks, storewomen and teleprinter operators. No good – I couldn't type. The WAAF needed drivers. My driving wasn't all that good, and I'd have preferred the Army. And a day or two ago the ATS had appealed for girls to do something that really sounded up my street.

Should I? Should I?

My teaching career had begun on 1 August last year: 1940. But after only five weeks, it had stopped. Seventeen of East Ham's forty-odd schools were destroyed or damaged in that first weekend of the Blitz. All schools were closed and new evacuation plans for children and mothers-with-babies were hurriedly put into operation. For twelve weeks, nothing but train journeys into the unknown, the children carefully labelled like parcels, a trench-warfare-type postcard in their pockets to send home; and a churn of milk in each railway carriage. It was the best that could be done. It was heart-breaking.

After Christmas, school began again, for the children who had stayed or who had come back, in what premises could be found.

The bus lurched, and stopped. No romantic Romeo came to sit by me; only Mr Harris. It was June, and it was raining.

I thought: I'll join the Army, if Mr Harris says …

'Flaming June, eh?' he remarked, as he thumped himself down.

That was it. Mr Harris had made my decision.

My spirits lifted. Of course. To do a man's job. Maths, an outdoor life, something to help improve our anti-aircraft defences. Teaching? Work of national importance? I was more like a walking national disaster. Fond of the children, individually, and they of me; but manage a class? Nothing could I learn, and nothing teach. But here was something made for me. Something I could be capable of. To help the guns' performance, in their defence of my country.

Mr Harris was talking to me.

'Yes,' I answered. Oh, yes!

Mathematical qualifications, good eyesight, good general health, love of open-air life …

'Oh, yes. I agree.'

'Kine', as in 'kinema'. Kine-theodolite operator. Interesting work, to help combat the bombing of our cities.

'Of course!'

I skipped along the road to the school, dodging the rain-filled incendiary holes. There would be two more months, which the office required as notice. Already I was regretting leaving my class, but I could not expect to keep them for ever.

It was almost a pleasure, saying 'Good morning' to my bugbear, the headmaster, and signing the attendance book before he could draw his red line.

But truly the issue had been brooding in my mind for a long time, and the bubble that had burst in my brain had been growing more and more intolerable. War was no longer the business of fighting troops alone: every man, woman and child was part of it now.

Even the flowers in the garden had had to make their sacrifices. Only war could have turned my father's garden into a Robinson Crusoe's island. He and my mother had just added a goat to the menagerie out there. There were chickens in the rose bower, rabbits in the summer house; and now, a goat. Only a year ago, in the world as it had been, my mother had still been living the life of a lady, in the bungalow that she had designed herself, keeping house with the money that my father earned, having tea with friends and giving parties. When I came down from college last summer, instead of a mother I found a full-time air-raid warden. Full trousered uniform, tin hat, police whistle and brass bell. She loved it. Out in the real world, doing her bit. She had even grown taller. Four feet ten, at least. And being paid £2 per week.

My father was spending nearly every night up in the City, where he worked on Lloyd's Shipping Index. His night 'ship' began at ten o'clock, but he always left the house early, to be in time for a few hours' firefighting. All through that terrible winter, the sirens had sounded punctually at six o'clock, heralding wave after wave of incendiary raids, to light the targets for the high-explosive attacks, later in the night.

Daddy could always make us laugh. We laughed about

him playing football with incendiary bombs up on that City roof, trampolining on the wire mesh that had been stretched across the dome, and bouncing the things into the street; we laughed at his description of all the people he was meeting at Lloyd's these nights, playing billiards and eating in the hallowed Captains' Room.

But he came home in the mornings grey with fatigue and worry, not telling Mummy and me about the shipping losses he had been recording all night. Some mornings he did not come home at all, when the bombing was very bad. Staff were not allowed home for days together sometimes.

The Lutine Bell hung silent now. It was either that or have it ringing constantly. How can he have endured the worry of it all?

He had been there on that worst night of all, almost the last day of 1940. As far as the eye could see, there were fires, and the water supply had failed; even Lloyd's own artesian well was exhausted. He watched as whole buildings collapsed; he saw the lovely spires of old City churches flare like torches, incandesce, then fall. St Paul's itself was threatened on all sides, its dome now hidden by smoke, now lit by another flame, now dark again. And each time, all night, it was still there, as if by a miracle.

That is the night that everyone remembers. That is the night that was the worst, so far.

The next night the Lutine Bell broke its silence, just once. For the safe arrival of 1941.

Romford, where we lived, was on the bombers' flight path to London, and sometimes the raids were so heavy and the gunfire so intense that a lot of damage was done. It was not as bad as central London, but quite bad enough.

The land-mines were the worst. Swinging on their parachutes, they drifted gracefully, so slowly, the sky full of them sometimes, and the guns banging away at them all night.

'And we still can't hit them!'

One night the blast from one of them blew its dirt and debris through our house, into the shelter where we were, then sucked it all back again, taking the breath out of us as it did so. My mother had to go on duty at midnight that night, and the warden she was relieving was in the post, shaking and crying.

'I couldn't save him. Why couldn't I save him?'

He had found a man in the ruins of a house, still alive, sprawled across the smashed lavatory pan he had been sitting on. Half his behind had been blown away, and the warden had tried to staunch the fountain of blood with a field dressing, but the man had died.

'He was still alive when I found him. Why couldn't I save him?' he said, again and again.

He never got over the shock of it. He remained a warden and performed his duties, but he became morose, speaking only the words required by the drill book.

The air-raid wardens had been prepared for the expected invasion. The instructions for Romford were: 'We are on the main route to London. German troops will need to stop their march from time to time and come into the houses for food. Tell your neighbours to leave some in the house, but when the Red Alert comes, get all the people into the gardens. Prepare a store of food in your air-raid shelter. Open the front doors and lock the back. There's no virtue in being a hero for no reason.'

Hence the goat.

The only duty that really upset my mother was having to fit babies with gas masks. Every baby that was born had to be introduced to the contraption, put into it, and the mother instructed how to pump the filtered air into it. Mummy had said, 'That's all very well, but what about milk for the babies?' The mother might be killed or the shock dry her milk, and you couldn't sterilize Cow & Gate in the furtive dark, on a spirit stove.

Binky was very pretty, with critical eyes and a stripy face; a wicked sense of humour, like all goats. But alas! She proved to be only five months old, and she also proved my town-bred parents' abysmal ignorance of the facts of life. They were disappointed, naturally, to discover how young she was, but still thought that all that was necessary was patience, and the milk would arrive in time. There she was, now, tethered on the little lawn near the house, bleating to be taken for a walk and to be fed. Who wanted a house-trained goat that didn't know what grass was for?

Mercifully, mercifully, the invasion had not taken place.

But what was I doing? Nothing. Part-time air-raid warden. What was that? The wardens at the post all treated me like a child and gave me the safe jobs. Only once had I had something even half-interesting to do.

I helped to test the anti-gas outfit. Air-tight oilskins, tin hat and respirator. Walk all round the block. My companion was a lady of uncertain age: a trim little sandy-haired body. The walk was surprisingly difficult and unpleasant, but we made it. I felt hot and horrible, but she was near collapse. When she tore off her gas mask, I gasped. She was not herself. What had happened? Her face was in ruins. Wrinkled, streaked and discoloured. Her eyes were two black blotches, and her mouth had lost its shape. She looked old. No: she looked her age. All her pretences were gone.

This was the reality of war. We all faced death or mutilation with whatever courage we could muster, and sometimes even dreamed of being heroic, but would one die half-undressed, as the man on the lavatory had, still on the smashed mess underneath him, or suffer like my gas-mask companion, who had to go on living with her neighbours, with all her dignity stripped from her? What was happening to our world? Where were the romantic images?

If there *was* something that could be done, I wanted to be part of it. I longed for some call from My Country. 'Your Country Needs YOU!' the old poster had said. If London ever needed me, I was ready. But the trap was closing, to hold me back in a job that I was no good at. What could I do?

It was a few weeks after this, after a week or two without raids, that the BBC had broadcast the ATS appeal for kine-theodolite operators, who were wanted for secret and essential work and who would be attached to the Royal Artillery.

The ATS recruiting sergeant was impatient: 'Teaching's a reserved occupation. You're wasting my time.'

'Only from twenty-five years old, I'm sure.'

'Ah, yes, here it is. Only till September, though. You'll

have to be quick.' She said that I couldn't take the oath till I'd resigned, and to come back later.

'Have you any information about the job?'

She ferreted about and came up with a pamphlet which showed girls in navy blue skirts and white tops, at the fuze-testing beach at Shoeburyness.

'There's a note here. It says they want to expand the job, something to do with gunnery. Anti-aircraft. A technical job. A bit hush-hush.' She looked at me. 'And you've got to be at least five foot two tall.'

My hair's long, I thought. A nice hard bun on top, I thought.

'You'll be doing a man's job.'

And so it turned out to be. At the end of the 'emergency', and we were all demobbed, the work was taken back by men. That, of course, is why no one has ever heard of us. There have never been any WRAC kines: we disappeared. There was no need for our work, once the war was over.

The chief education officer himself came into my classroom, my resignation letter in his hand. But I had already taken the oath, on my way home from posting the letter, and was immune to blandishments.

'I'm glad it was the Army you chose,' said my dad. He seemed not at all surprised. My mother kissed me. 'It's only what I would have done, at your age.'

Germany invaded the Soviet Union. Goodness, that made Red Russia our ally! 'Our gallant Russian allies,' we all quipped. But it was good to know that someone else was standing up to the Nazis.

In the lull, Daddy was busy again. Our garden air-raid shelter was letting in water. It must have been damaged by that late land-mine. He bought a cottage. That is, he bought the frame timbers of an old cottage that Wackett's were demolishing, and the roof tiles, too. He had a scheme for turning my bedroom into a fortress. Steel shutters at the windows, a few tons of sand between the joists in the loft, and the room itself lined with the old oak frame to shore up the ceiling.

'You won't want to spend another winter in that shelter in the garden.'

It smote me for the first time that my mother would be left alone at night in any coming trouble.

'Natural advantage of a bungalow,' he remarked, smugly. 'No one else along here can do this.'

'What did you buy the tiles for?' my mother asked.

'10 bob,' he replied.

'No ...'

'Well, I thought they might come in useful for something.'

He fitted the old timbers into the room, sawing great holes in the floor to stand them firm, and he and I had a busy day or two, carrying two yards of sand up the ladder, into the loft.

2 'Squad, Shun!'

Talavera Camp, Northampton: September 1941

The great thing about Army basic training is that it leaves you with life-long confidence. If you survive it, nothing in the way of discomfort, humiliation, culture-shock or fatigue that life can bring afterwards can be as bad. It is worse than the first form of a public school. It carries a two-pronged mental attack. It does this deliberately, for the same reasons, and it has the same effects. My teacher training made me aware of the psychology of it, but even so I could not resist what it was doing to me.

All the humiliations take place during the first week. The very first shock is latrine parade, when you first arrive. Our squad, who were not yet a squad, lined up at the front of the hut to which we had been directed. It was one of eight, built near a group of brick-built blocks. The twenty-four of us shuffled into some sort of group.

'Squad – move to the right in threes. Quick march! Left right left right left right left. Right wheel …' and so on, till we were at the back of the hut instead of the front.

We were sent off in sixes, to use the latrines. The Army uses no euphemisms. One poor girl in the third group exceeded the allotted minute. The corporal went in after her, and we could hear the shouting from where we stood. No opportunity to wash hands, the ablutions block being the adjacent one, and this was not ablutions parade.

Hundreds – thousands – of young women were responding to the nation's call, and there were 200 in our company, all of whom had arrived that day. Every fortnight, another 200. And this was only one of several training camps.

The second smack in the face was the impersonal nature of the issuing of personal kit, and of bedding. Everything was public property, stamped with the royal cypher and the date of manufacture. Flung at us by the orderly in charge came jackets and skirts, two of each; vests, two sorts of pants, bras, suspender belts, stockings, ties, cap, kitbag, woollen gloves, woolly jumper, pyjamas. Shirts, greatcoat, groundsheet cape, waterproof; overalls, working women's.

Khaki is not a becoming colour.

'Put your stuff into the kitbag, and come over this side.'

Into the bag went cap badge, buttonstick, shoes, shoebrushes 1 and 2, shoelaces, gymshoes, field dressing, fork, knife, spoon, mug, towels, brass-cleaner, brass button brush, hairbrush, toothbrush, comb and housewife. Housewife, pronounced 'hussif,' a nice little roll-up mending kit, even to the thimble, and tied up with two bows – khaki, of course.

'Sign here!'

At a separate table sat a sergeant, who doled out our identity discs as we signed.

Back to the hut with that lot, then to the blanket store. Some of us were pretty tired by now.

Three blankets, two pillows, two sheets, two pillowslips. We did not have to carry the mattresses. They had already been put on the iron beds.

Parade again. More shouting. Left right left right left right left. The PAD store. ('Passive something Defence'. Or 'Personal'?) Service gas mask and its haversack; eyeshields; anti-dim; cases eyeshields, one; ointment, anti-gas, pots, one; ear-plugs.

'Get your bed made up, and outside here again in ten minutes.'

There was a table set out in front of the hut, with a complete kit arranged on it. A corporal explained each item of it to us, and how we were to put it on.

Another shock. Out there, in the open camp, for anyone to see, she held out a rather intimate garment.

'Here's your brassière.' She made it sound like a fire. 'If it doesn't fit, you've got your hussif. Make it fit before morning parade tomorrow. Turn your stocking tops over when you attach the suspenders. Don't put the suspenders on the thin bit and expect to get replacements when they ladder. If they ladder, you'll have to mend them. You only get new stockings from stores when they're worn out, with visible darns. This is how to tie a tie.'

Well, that at least was easy. It's the same as the girdle of a gym tunic. But then, how many of these girls had ever worn a gym tunic? She told us how to lace our shoes, and then the most incredible thing happened.

The ATS corporal held up, in the open, two packets of something. 'These are issued every month. One packet. Size 2. If you want size 1 or 3, you'll ask your corporal.'

We all nearly died of shame. There were men walking around the camp: the drill sergeants whom we were to meet tomorrow, and other men. It was shameful. Nobody talked about such things, openly. Even in chemists' shops, they were not displayed on open shelves: you waited till no male customers or children were in earshot, and whispered to the assistant, who brought them out from a dark cupboard.

'Oh – before you break off. Put on your identity discs. Wear them round your neck. They're never to be taken off, whatever you're doing.' This was a joke, and a snigger went round the squad. 'They've got your name, number and religion. If they have to be used, one goes to your next-of-kin, and one stays on the body. Then they know which way to bury you.'

She showed us the regulation way to lace up shoes, and dismissed us to go into the hut and get it all on. We fell out, groaned our way into the hut and folded our individuality into our suitcases, for the duration.

The permanent staff at Talavera Camp were mostly men. The orderly room, general stores, motor transport, medical reception centre. There were a few ATS junior officers, and the squad corporals were girls, but the drill sergeants were men, and so were all the senior ranks.

Our drill sergeant was a man indeed, and every inch a soldier. He had his part to play in the breaking of our spirit. But the drilling I quite enjoyed. It was a relaxation to me, watching someone else giving the orders, and having the chance to be the naughty boy myself, if I chose.

'Pick up yer dressing! No – leave yer clothes alone! I don't want ter see yer drawers. I'll see better than them tonight. Squad – squad, shun!'

'Keep yer faces straight: eyes front. Don't look at me, and keep yer faces straight. EYES – FRONT!'

'Come here, Curly Locks. Oh, what lovely curls! Get that cut by tomorrow. Two inches off the collar, understand?'

'Squad – open order. March!' and he would go through a mime of going mad and appealing to Heaven.

We were not to be allowed out of camp until Sunday.

'If you're smart enough, you can go on church parade. I can't see you making it, though.'

It was the evenings in the canteen that I dreaded most. These girls were not like anyone I had ever encountered before. Rough Cockneys I could have coped with; basic Essex or tough Kentish would at least have been familiar; but by some quirk all the girls except myself and one other, a girl called Ira, were from Midland areas that were completely foreign to me. Their sense of humour lacerated me. They had mostly been in domestic service of some sort and had been trained to a superficial subservience and politeness, but their off-duty conversation was unbelievable.

We all have our allergies: insect bites, cats, pollen or dust; but my allergy is to ugly words, filthy jokes with no wit, and horrible voices. I can't help it. No cure has ever been found for it. That fortnight nearly killed me. My shyness did not help.

I tried to be friendly: 'What do you want to be?' I asked a group of them at table, on the second day.

'Officer's groundsheet – that's what she wants to be – eh, eh?' Raucous laughter. Their worst remarks have been Freudianly suppressed out of my memory. To me they said, 'How about you? What you joined this lot up for? Bloody officer?'

The term 'kine-theodolite' seemed to ignite a spark that swept all round the mess hall, and mincing imitations of my reply haunted me for days.

Ira was going to be a driver, and she came in for some of their ribaldry, too.

The Navy, Army and Air Force Institute's canteen – the NAAFI – was the only place to spend the evening, confined as we were to the camp. It was either that or stay in the hut. The NAAFI cook was a man, and he liked to come to the counter and take the orders himself. He had his own style of flirtation and considered himself a wit. He had more disgusting puns for every item of food on the menu than I would have thought possible. My misery was my own fault. I should have laughed with the others, to hide myself in the crowd, but found myself cringing with embarrassment. One of their tricks was to misconstrue what anyone said, put an obscene construction on it, then repeat it, at the tops of their voices.

'Oh, look! She's blushing! She must have a dirty mind!'

It was sheer hell. And we were chained together, day and night, for at least a week. I longed that we should be smart enough to parade on Sunday and be allowed out of the camp in the evenings next week.

But I was not the only one who was suffering. These very foul-mouthed girls with no apparent shame were very disturbed by the total lack of personal privacy. They washed little bits of themselves surreptitiously, shocked by the rows of washbasins with no screen at all; and they undressed as secretly as they could. It is not pleasant for any young girl to be suddenly robbed of a little corner to call her own, and it was unpleasant for us all, but at least I had had to come to terms with it years before, at school, undressing for a shower in the changing-room, and this was not so much worse.

By the fifth day we had had another medical. One girl, on closer inspection, had proved to be not exactly female and had been discharged; two pathetic little things who had sobbed in each other's arms all night were discovered in bed together the next morning and had been shipped off in disgrace somewhere, and three recruits had come to fill the spaces.

There had been dental inspection and some treatment. TT and TAB jabs, with permission to take forty-eight hours off duty, though not the opportunity; foot inspection after three days; and kit inspection.

This last proved very interesting. It is not too easy to keep a decent change of clothes with only two or three of everything. Seven items of laundry could be sent once a week, and there was a drying-room for our own dabbling-out. I had a pair of damp pants and a damp, unironed shirt when the inspection was called.

The three girls next to me were railed at for the bad condition of their display: they had gone through all their stuff, and it was all dirty and crumpled at the bottom of their kitbags. The ones who received the highest praise had nearly everything perfect – brand new, in fact. There is nothing like living in the same shirt, twenty-four hours a day, for having a nice set of kit to show.

And all the time, the noise outside. Bugle calls, and the shouting. Male voices barking, snapping and roaring, and a few female corporals and young officers, mostly feeble and shrill. Here and there a bell-like boom ensured the owner's rapid promotion.

Bullied, praised, cajoled and slammed. No coughing on parade; no sneezing. Noses are not allowed to run.

'Keep yer 'ands still! Eyes front! Hup two three four, down two three four, about two three four.' Nobody bothered to explain that this was saluting drill for pay parade.

The final spirit-crusher was tailor-made for me, and anyone like me. We had to don the overall, working woman's. Shapeless, stiff as a board, half-inch-thick blue denim. I was determined not to be defeated, and tried to cheer up. Tying a string around my middle, I paraded in something that looked like a dowager's crinoline. The task was to scrub. It was an enormous space, with a concrete floor. In line abreast we scrubbed, for what seemed like hours. There was one more move to make, and then it would be done.

Then the company sergeant major came to inspect. Where such an immaculate man found mud to put on his boots, goodness knows, but he came and walked on the wet bit we had just finished, strode the whole length of it, told us we might have to do it all again the next morning, said, 'You'd better do this bit again. It's dirty' – and left.

Some of the girls cried.

And all these delights were interspersed with the meals. Two large swill tubs stood at either end of the hatch, where we had to queue for our food, and all the scrapings went into them. Fat and gristle, custard, fish ears, gravy, bits of burnt jam, all went in. Tired as we were, homesick as we were, aching as we were, and every hour or so, back on the drill parade, it was not easy. Serve your country? Hold on to the thought, if you possibly can.

Marching drill, marking time, turning about, wheeling and assembling and dressing from a marker. On Saturday morning we were declared not fit for tomorrow's parade through the town. And there was not a private corner to cry in.

That afternoon a new sergeant came and put us through a manoeuvre or two.

'You're beginning to get the feel of it,' he declared. 'We'll see.'

Wretched man. Wretched Army. I knew what they were up to.

On Sunday we went on church parade, marching through the streets to a drum-and-fife band. Of course. And our company was told that it was the best intake they had ever had. Of course.

The second week did not feel so bad. The unbleached cotton bed-sheets were just as rough, the latrines and ablutions just as cold and wet, and just as unpleasant to clean when your turn came; September dews were just as cold at 6.30 in the morning, the swill tub just as revolting; but our blisters were healing, the dentist had finished with us, we were hungry enough to eat without thinking too much, we had had all the injections, and we could go out of camp in the evenings.

We were beginning to feel not quite so raw: the tailor had taken up hems and fitted sleeves and taken in waists; we had rubbed the newness off our caps, bent our cap badges just so, and so; the brass was beginning to shine, our shoes were getting softer, and we were beginning to swagger.

On Monday we had to do an intelligence test. Now I was in my element: a room full of desks, an examination paper before me, and a pencil. A picture test, choosing the right shape to match or balance or mirror the one at the end; then a page or two of choosing the right squiggle to complete the required shape. The last two pages were simple mathematical series to continue. Warm and comfortable, and no one shouting at you. I was like the cat who had been at the cream.

Ira and I went to the cinema that evening and had to remember to say 'Friend!' when challenged at the gate. Real soldiers! The late-night barrack-room conversation did not seem to matter so much.

More drill next day, but now becoming almost satisfying. Slow march. That was my favourite. We were taught it by a Royal Artillery sergeant: a very dramatic style, the RAs. And turning on the march: you are marching along, then, when the order is given, 'One, two, three, four!', you are marching in the opposite direction. Very nifty.

Lectures: military law; documents; crime and punishment; And all about messing. This last lecture taught us a dozen ways to avoid wasting fat – disgusting, from start to finish.

Then we had to assemble in the big hall of the camp, for a talk by the regimental sergeant major. The colonel might be the CO, but the RSM was the truly Great Man of the camp. His voice and presence were everywhere.

'Now,' he boomed, 'you all think you're going home on leave at the end of the week, don't you? Well, I can tell you, you'll only get leave when you're posted to your unit. And you can't go to your unit till your course comes up. We can't have cooks who can't cook feeding the troops, can we?' This was a joke, and we obediently groaned. 'So don't come weeping and wailing to me, saying you want your mum. Look at me!'

(Oh, no, I thought. Now we're going to get the 'now you're grown up' bit. It's going to be more of a carbon copy of teacher training than I thought. 'You are now adult. You say you love your parents. Nonsense. You only love the source of warmth and food. Love? You don't know what the word means.' He's going to tell us to grow up, and bully us.)

He went on: 'Take a look at me. I've been in the Army for twenty years. The Army made a man of me. And I'll tell you this: I'm still homesick, and I want my mum!'

Oh.

'There's nothing I'd like better than to be at home with her right now. But we're in this Army to fight Hitler. Remember Hitler? You've been too busy these last few days to think about him, much. But he's waiting for us. We're going to finish him, together, you and me. We haven't got time for a few months to cry for mum.'

I took a deep breath. The trick – the double-pronged assault – had worked. I felt the warmth spread through me. I was lost. I belonged to something greater than myself. Love and loyalty. Just like first form. Alternate bullying and praise; pushing to the limit of endurance with threats and insults, then a kind word. I knew what they were doing. But it still worked. Only a broken spirit can love.

The ATS badly needed officers and senior NCOs to take over from the men and train ATS by ATS, and the selection officer sent for me.

'You were a teacher.'

'Yes, Ma'am.'

'You have applied for kine-theodolite operator.'

'Yes.'

'I have selected you to go instead to OCTU and train as an officer, because we need female officers to train the recruits, instead of having to rely on the men.'

Yuk! I thought. Stay here? Teacher's job, on orderly's pay? No thanks.

'I joined up especially to do that particular job. It was teaching I left.' She looked as though she might bite me, so I added, 'I want to go on the trade course first, and then perhaps I could see about OCTU afterwards.'

'You won't stand a chance,' she told me. 'You haven't a degree. You have to be a BSc to be a kine-theodolite officer.'

The die, as they say, was cast. I had chucked away my chance to take the King's Commission, to meet more interesting people, to live in reasonable comfort and wear something one degree more becoming. And my parents would have been pleased. But I had set my heart on doing something that was within my capabilities. And if the barrack-room company was rough, I'd have to put up with it.

There was no kine course for three weeks, so I stayed at Talavera Camp, attended Ira's motor transport course with her, saw her off, spent a week in the orderly room sorting documents, saw my own intelligence test papers and result (Golly!) and, searching through them all, found another name with full marks. Valerie Cox, with an address in London; and she, too, was headed for the kine-theodolite course. I could not wait to meet her.

After a day or two I was given an office of my own, next door to the RSM, and soldiers kept coming in, thinking that it was still empty. I made a notice and nailed it up on my door.

His notice read: 'RSM.'

Mine said, 'PRIVATE.'

From his lofty rank, he allowed me to hear him laugh at my little joke.

3 'Cheer up, Sunshine'

Train Journey to Manorbier, October 1941

Getting across London, in this time of war, was no problem. I had been spared the fag of the underground, and the expense of a taxi.

Day and night, outside every main-line station there was a fleet of coaches. They were camouflaged a dull green and were for the use of the forces. They linked all the termini and were there for anyone travelling on duty. You just stepped on, rode the rounds and got off at the station you wanted. It was a wonderful service, and free of charge to all ranks.

At the stations there were also the railway transport officers. Any travelling problem they would help you with, and I found myself looking for the RTO armband on stations for years afterwards. Probably not cost-effective, in these days.

Paddington Station. Now you're a soldier. A self-contained unit, travelling alone. Railway warrant and a man's-type kitbag. What an unwieldy object! A leaden sausage it is, vying with the service gas mask, to be a common danger. Remember, when it is on your shoulder, not to swing round suddenly when there are people about.

'Don't come to me if you lose your gas mask,' the sergeant had said. 'Pinch someone else's before you come crying to me.'

Self-reliant, now. On your own.

I was bound for a place called Manorbier, in South Wales. That is where the KT establishment was. What a place to spend the war! Some Welsh coal-tip, miles away from nowhere. The only things I knew about South Wales were the coal-dust and the misery. *How Green Was My Valley* and *The Corn Is Green*. And Cronin, of course. What a prospect!

Paddington Station stank of fish. Empty boxes were being loaded into a train a few platforms away. Ah, here was Platform 1, and a train about a mile long. And such crowds! A porter – that's what I wanted. I offered my florin, thinking it was over-generous. Sixpence or a shilling were more usual, or so I thought. But times had changed:

He flung it back at me. 'Don't you know there's a war on? If that's all yer got, you better keep it.' And he left my bag on the platform. I dared not drag it: it was only made of canvas.

'Cheer up, Sunshine!' Some soldiers had got hold of a porter's trolley and loaded all their stuff onto it. 'Who needs porters? There's room for a little one on top.' They took the bag for me, all the way to the front of the train.

Oh, yes. I wasn't a rookie, any more.

This, of course, meant that I had no choice of carriage, and I was a little nervous of being the only girl among a lot of men. And common soldiers, at that. As a section of society, they had always had a bad name: the lowest form of human life. Whether he is a cavalry trooper, an infantry private or an artillery gunner, he will not work unless chivvied, will not keep himself clean unless bullied and gets drunk whenever he can. And here I was, in a nest of them.

They were chatty – and inquisitive: 'How long you been in this lot?'

'Oh – a little while.' It was shameful, to admit being a rookie.

'What do you do in Civvy Street?'

Every teacher knows that there is nothing so calculated to kill conversation stone dead as to admit the awful truth.

'I – er – I took children into the country, evacuation ...' I half-lied.

They laughed when I told them about being told off for wasting public money. My first trip had been to Castle Ashby near Northampton, where I had had twelve children to place, including a French boy who spoke no English and who wanted to find an empty cottage that his mother could rent, and bring the little brothers and sisters. It had taken me four days to settle them to my satisfaction, and the woman who had taken me in was the wife of the marquis's ex-valet, who was old now and a bed-ridden invalid. She could not cope with children but looked after me very kindly.

'I don't know what they've brought you here for,' she said. 'We've had a bomb.'

'Last night?'

'No – two or three weeks ago. Come and see.' She pointed out of the little window. 'It fell over there.'

I could see nothing. 'Oh, you can't really see it. But it wasn't far away. Only about four miles.'

She was a sweet, kind woman, and she charged me, for four days' full board, even knowing that I should be reimbursed, 10 shillings.

And the office told me off, for wasting public money! I should have left the children in the hands of the billeting officer, whose job it was, and come home the next morning. I went to tell the children's mothers where they were and what the place was like, and was told off for that, too. I was supposed to be on school premises or at the town hall during school hours. So I had to wait until after four o'clock to tell the last two.

The train stopped, and one or two of the soldiers got up and looked up and down the platform. Apparently there was nothing of interest, and they came back.

'Taff! Where's Taff?' The Welshman had disappeared. 'Where's he to?' 'I can't see him, look you!' 'Look you, Taffy, where are you to?'

One of the other men, a young shy lad, who had not joined in their conversations, slipped out onto the station.

Taffy returned with tea for us all, on an improvised tray. He had discovered the WVS tea-trolley, further up the platform. Good old Taff!

The quiet boy came back, with a cup of tea in his hand.

'Pull up the ladder, Jack! I'm all right!' was their taunt.

He was shy: I could see that. I suffered the same way, and knew how he must have felt. He was not particularly selfish, just afraid of pushing himself forward. He was ignored for the rest of the journey.

But I was learning. I felt emboldened to ask questions myself.

'Where do you live?' I asked Taffy.

'Bridgend. Do you know it?'

'No – but I've heard of it. Some friends of mine went there.'

I had heard of it. In all the early London bombing, only three East Ham children had been killed. They were two sisters and their brother, evacuated to Bridgend almost at the beginning of the Blitz. The billeting officer had been considerate to them, finding two adjoining houses, one for the girls and one for the boy. They had been there two days when a bomb demolished both houses, killing everyone in them.

'You've had some bombing there, as well,' I said.

'Yes, it was bad.'

Conversation became general again, and then they wanted to know more about the evacuation journeys. I told them about the journey to Ely, where the WVS had done us all proud, organizing a marvellous meal, but before we knew what was happening, the billeting officer loaded the children onto coaches and refused to tell us, their escorts, where they were going. No arrangements had been made for us to stay anywhere: they assumed that we would go straight back to London, that night.

'Don't you know there's a Blitz on?'

Now, there is one way to find out where a coach is going: ask the driver. So the next morning found one of the other women and me taking the bus out to where our children were and knocking on doors all round the village: 'Have you got one of the London children who arrived yesterday?'

What a life.

'Bloody officials,' one of my companions remarked. 'Oh – beg your pardon, Miss.'

After some sandwiches, out came the beer. They offered me some before drinking all there was, and settled down to sleep, leaving me to my thoughts. Now, there was a strange thing! I had dreaded the rough behaviour and the rougher conversation that I had been sure would be my lot, for this ride into the unknown, and had found nothing but kindness and good company. Perhaps it was only women, in mass, who were so horrible.

Never mind, never mind. Everything turns out in the end. And surely it was better than that awful staff-room, with the horrible head, and the master with the hairy toes who warmed my tea-cup for me and called me his little bluebird!

I had no more stories to tell. There was no story in the trip to Norwich, where the organization was superb, even to getting the train to stop opposite a big modern brick-and-glass school which had been turned into a gigantic reception centre. There was every amenity imaginable, including a good meal for everyone. People who were going to be the host families came, while we were eating, and it was more like a party than the usual sad sorting-out.

And I could not tell them about the other extreme: that dreadful place in Cornwall, beyond St Austell, beyond everywhere, it had seemed to us, after the interminable journey. Here there was no organization at all. The children were herded off the train, in a strange place, in the dark, and offered no food, no drink, not even (God help us!) a lavatory.

We have all read accounts about the filthy slum children, coming to live in the sweet country air. Anyone would be filthy after that day's ordeal, smelly from the steam train, sticky from sweets, and tear-stained, nervous and homesick. If they were not damp where they should not have been damp when we got off the train, many were, and worse, by the time they had been kept waiting, lined up in the gloomy half-lit village hall for half-an-hour, waiting for the lady of the manor to come and take first pick, before the rest of the village women, in descending social order, came to choose.

Dirty slum children? They were dirty, all right. Sick and frightened. What I saw that night ought to have turned me off my sentimental Londoner's dream of living in a village, for ever. No, I couldn't tell my soldier companions about that.

The train went on and on. Past all sign of civilization, past all clues as to where we were. Change at Whitland. And off again.

The last stage of the journey was by three-ton lorry.

'Put your foot in that hole, love. Up you go!'

It was dark, and late. An ATS officer was marshalling all the khaki-clad girls she could see, and there was female chatter around me.

There was a meal ('Get your irons out!') and a five-minute march to a big wooden hut. Blankets and sheets were on the beds, all ready for us: all we had to do was make them up. Then a bath; what bliss! Wash away the smutty, steamy train smell. Then the bugle call sounded. Everyone into barracks.

What power it has, the Last Post, even though it is a daily routine, sounding in the night air across a hushed camp where only the sentries are out, on duty. My already homesick soul was ready for tears, without that. I was glad to delay getting back into the hut until nearly Lights Out.

There were nineteen of us, nearly all strangers to one another, having come from all the training camps in the country. Cox, Valerie, was here, though I had not seen her on the train. None of us had had much to say to one another yet: we were all tired and probably all cautious, after our recent experiences.

I lay there in the dark, trying to sleep. What would tomorrow bring? This was what it was all about: keep hold of that thought. Be brave. You're helping to fight for your country; for your city. If it means more of that sort of hateful company and more coarseness and dirty conversation, you'll have to put up with it. Go to sleep.

Then, quietly, someone began singing. The girl in the bed nearly opposite mine was crooning in the dark. Something familiar.

'My love dwelt in a northern land; a dark tower in a forest green was hi-is, and far away ...'

And softly, very softly, we all took it up, each remembering the song we had all learned in our choirs in our various schools. It is impossible to describe the sensation we all felt: it was as if we had all come home. We were of the same sort: we had found one another. I was not the only one who wept in joy and thankfulness that night. It was Rita Williams, as she then was, who had begun the singing.

This was not the only type of song we had in common. In the days that followed, all the boarding-school uggies came out, the silly mock-folk-songs, morbid camp-fire horrors, as well as more choral specials.

And we had left the worst of barrack-room language behind. It was not that we never swore: we did, and colourfully. But it was like pepper in our conversation, not lard.

4   'Target – Plane – Observe!'

Kine Course, Manorbier, October 1941

In Germany, people do not go to the cinema: they go to the *kinema*. And that explains why we were going to be 'kine-theodolite' operators, not 'cine-theodolite' operators. The junior commander instructor, who wore a red band round her cap, invited half of us to come out of our desks and have a closer look at the kine. It had a German brand name. 'Bambergwerk,' it said. That took some swallowing. Why were we to use a German instrument? Couldn't we make our own?

It was essentially a cine- (kine-) camera. Sergeant Major Lorna Parkes picked up a black cassette and pulled out the tail of film: 35 mm film. If we had been the old sweats that we were to become very soon, our first reaction would have been: 'Who's got a 35-mm camera?' But we were innocent still, on that day, and thought nothing of the kind. The 100-foot stock cassette was placed in the camera, and she showed us how to feed the end round all the sprockets and fix it into the take-up container and put that in its place, checking the film loops. She tapped a key that was on the table, and the film took up. Click. Single shot. Another tap, another click. She swung the thing round on its base ring, which was marked in degrees, all round the circle.

Evelyn Cochrane was a good teacher. In that sudden snowstorm of technical and scientific words that descended on us for the three weeks of the course, she led us calmly into a clear sight of what we were trying to do, and how.

The kine is a very cunning instrument. It fixes a moving

object in time as well as space. The ordinary theodolite that surveyors use is all right for field corners or church steeples or anything else that is prepared to stay still, but for an aircraft the problem is different.

Here are the bones of what we learned.

To fix the point in space of any object that can be seen, two kines are needed, one at each end of a surveyed line, about three miles long.

When they look at each other, they call that 0 degrees on their horizontal rings; and when they turn to look at something else, the angles of turn can be read off the rings, and a triangle imagined. The apex of the triangle is where the object is; or rather, the point on the ground underneath the object. The triangle's base is the three miles between the kines.

There is also the upper half of a vertical ring on the instrument, also marked in degrees; and when the lens is elevated, another triangle can be plotted: kine to target; target down to the ground, and along back to the kine. You have two kines, so there are two different side triangles. And on this information, everything is based.

The kine-theodolite not only observes: it records. It not only photographs the target, which might be an aeroplane or a sleeve or flag towed behind that aeroplane: it also records, in the top corners of each frame, a portion of the bearing ring with its pointer, and the corresponding bit of the vertical ring.

If you link the two instruments electrically, both camera shutters can be operated from a central control post at the same instant. A very pretty instrument.

You can take the film home, develop it, read the angles through a magnifying evaluator and, by calculating with a lot of sines, cosines, tans and other mysteries, fix that target in time and space. And if your guns are firing, you can read off and calculate the position of the shell-bursts and find out their displacement, with absolute accuracy.

Some of us were disappointed to learn that our work could not be used in action: our results took hours to produce. It was intended for practice firing, to help the gun teams assess their faults and correct them.

Much of the course took place indoors. We were taught

a bit of practical trigonometry and introduced to the seven-figure log book and the circular slide rule – 'the lavatory seat', as everyone called it; enough optics to choose the right lens, fit a prism and choose the right film and colourfilter; enough electricity to be able to assemble and use a field telephone and adjust its buzzer, to link up six-volt batteries in various ways; and to use the kine-theodolite. The little bit of physics we were taught was a revelation to some of us: many girls' schools, in those days, had no physics classes. I, for one, found a whole world I had never suspected. But there was no time – no time.

'You realize,' Lorna said to us, one day, 'that the real kine course takes three months. We have three weeks. You'll have to work hard.'

It was stimulating. It was fun. It wasn't easy. And it was all so hasty. There wasn't time to exercise the soldier's time-honoured right to grumble. And we had to learn the Army's way of doing things, As Laid Down In The Drill Book.

TO COME INTO ACTION

No.1	No.2	No.3
Sees that correct filter and lens are used. Fits pentagonal prism.	Removes protector cap and fits ray shade.	Connects up telephone and terminal board (with 4th cable).
	Takes out cables and hands them to No. 1.	
Fits cables: Theodolite to switch-box.		
Switch box	hands to No.2	to battery cable.
Switch box	hands to No. 3	to terminal board.

And the verbal drills. You mustn't say, 'Oh, look – there's a plane!' You say: 'Target – plane – observe!' And so on.

And all this, all the outside work, surrounded by weather. We never realized that there could be so much weather. It wasn't just wet or dry, hot or cold. It varied subtly, winds coming up out of nowhere in a mixture of uncomfortable temperatures and humidities: soft and damp or soft and sweet; gusty and irritating or stinging with sudden drops of rain; blisteringly hot one minute and misty chill the next. We could usually see Caldy Island, with its lighthouse, but if far-away Lundy were visible, watch out! The rain would start soon. And Pembrokeshire rain can be like no other. Swift and chill, and horizontal.

We soon saw that there was not a coal mine in sight. Only grass-clad cliffs and sea and sky – and rain. And sun, sometimes. When it shines, it really shines. Gloriously, beautifully, magnificently, revealing something like Paradise.

Each way along the coast was enchanting. Eastwards along the limestone cliffs, the turf was cropped by rabbits, and if you lay and looked closely at the vegetation, there were dozens of exquisite little flowering plants within your arms' grasp: sweetly pretty mini-daisies and ferns and bells and peaseblossoms, pink and yellow and mauve and white and orange and red; pimpernels and eye-bright; some that we knew and some that we didn't, all packed close in an emerald-green sward.

Our first impression of the camp itself, the School of Anti-Aircraft Defence, was its height from the sea. The cliffs here are 500 feet high, and the only access to the little sandy beach below was a roughly hewn, scary step-scramble, and an equally hairy climb up again.

The cliff path in the westward direction, towards Manorbier Bay, is more difficult to find than the other, the plants on the red sandstone growing more lush and wild: foxgloves and bugloss, bracken and brambles, with honeysuckle scrambling through it all. And here and there great masses of gorse with its incredibly heady perfume.

Which ever way we had to go, to 'B' Station on the close turf or 'A' Station among the sweet-smelling scrub, our route took us along what must be one of the most beautiful paths in Britain. Not that it had been made into a path when we were there: we had to find the ways.

A few of our number had had experience of this kind of terrain; many of us had not. It was love at first sight. Our spirits learned to go free, up on those cliffs. I learned to breathe, to be, to enjoy just being alive. To emerge from an over-protected childhood, an over-supervised school life and all the pressures to aspire, to excel, to compete, into the life of a private soldier, where all you had to do was keep out of trouble and think what you liked, was a liberation in itself.

Those of us who passed the test, we were told, were to stay at Manorbier and continue to be quartered in the antiquated wooden huts up near the cliff edge. Someone in the past had made some attempt to camouflage them, and the sweeping, sinuous designs on the three generously proportioned huts gave them their name: the Mae West huts. They had been made more comfortable before our time by covering the latrine, ablutions and bath blocks all under one roof, all accessible from the rear – the cliff side – of all three huts. And the water was usually hot.

My first distinguishing act was to break a mirror. It was a full-length glass, hanging behind a door in the recreation room.

'Oh, blink!' I said to myself. 'There goes all my pay for weeks, never mind the seven years' bad luck.' A very good start to my Army life.

When I confessed, our kine corporal, Margaret Frost ('Frosty'), said, 'Threepence a week barrack damages all round, till it's paid for.' I didn't have to pay for it myself? 'You're in the Army now.'

The girl who sat next to me in class was called Honor Pryor. 'Brewer!' 'Pryor!' Our names were similar, and we found ourselves laughing at the same things. We both liked sugar in our tea at that time, and one day, being at the end of the queue, we were offered only unsweetened – 'You're in the Army now!' Honor and I hit it off almost immediately of first meeting. We were the same age within three weeks, had a similar ironical sense of humour and liked doing the same things. She was a librarian.

We had begun shaking down with little groups of friends. Honor, Winn Goldson and I formed such a group. Winn was older than the rest of us. She admitted to thirty-two, stoically fighting back tears for her fiancé, killed in a car-crash. She was a teacher, but there was always something of a mystery about her. She was tense and puritanical, but to Honor and me she was almost maternal.

We did have an hour or two free most evenings, in spite of all the homework. There was no shortage of escorts to take us out, and Honor and I found ourselves making foursomes. A half-hour's walk to Lydstep, perhaps, drop in to Mrs Walter's café for a toast supper and a cup of tea, and stroll back again. Sometimes there was a NAAFI dance. Tickets cost 3 pence, and the beer flowed freely.

The weather turned colder, and one day, in the middle of tea, into our mess came Frosty. We were very impressed with our course corporal. Out at stations she had the habit of lighting her cigarette by shorting out one of the accumulator batteries and catching the spark. We thought that that was very sophisticated and daring. She also kept her crisply curling hair in a bubble-cut with a razor blade. She had dash. We admired her.

She came in and said, 'Two volunteers to get coal. You and you. The coal store's open. Only for five more minutes, though. You'll have to be quick.'

Val Cox, whose mother's cousin was General Ironside, knew about the Army. She quoted from King's Regulations: 'A soldier cannot be put on duty in the middle of his tea.' She refused to budge. This made it awkward for the rest of us. None of us wanted to be put down as a greaser, and we were tickled at the idea of having rights. Particularly as the tea was fairly eatable for once. Well, you can get used to baked beans. So we stood fast. Sat fast.

'It's mutiny!' Frosty cried.

We discovered later that we had punished ourselves. The coal store usually closed at five o'clock, when we were still on the gun-park, and here was our lucky chance, owing to the kindness of the bombardier in charge. Oh well, Sarn fairy, as some of us might have said.

Another right that the soldier has is to grumble. Clever psychology that, on the part of Authority. Nothing like grumbling to weaken the will-power. But it becomes an addictive habit.

We were not too unhappy about being posted back, all together again, though we probably found something to grouse at. After a week's leave and our first taste of the night-time South Wales train, we became the 6th KT Detachment. There were now well over a hundred kine-ATS, in practice camps at Twm Fanau, Ty-Croes, Burrow Head and Bude, and at a special hush-hush establishment at Aberporth, as well as the HQ at Manorbier. There were whispers and hints that our detachment had a Future, but no one as yet knew what.

Our trade test results depleted us a little, but those of us who had passed were now officially attached to the Royal Artillery, and we were given their brass gun to wear over our breast pocket, as well as the coveted white lanyard. We had already begun to feel separate from the 'General Duties' ATS, who seemed to us to exist only to make life difficult for us. And we were proud of our attachment to the real – the men's – Army.

We were beginning to get to know one another. Val Cox was the Character of our group. She was nearly twenty-seven and one of those people who knows everyone. Wherever you had been, Val would have met someone you knew. She kept us in fits of laughter all the time. Judy Hickman, her friend, had recently married Charles, the theatrical producer. Judy was economical with tales of her life, which sounded like a dream to most of us.

And there was Verona. Verona Loynston-Pickard, our tallest member. A joyous, energetic girl, full of laughter. The daughter of a clergyman, the rector of Shorncliffe in Kent, she was seventeen years old and straight from school.

Every group of young women has its glamour girls, and ours were the two Mollys, Tapp and Howell. They were always having dates with interesting-sounding men – civilians, mostly. We never discovered who the men were or where they had met them. They giggled together, sometimes drawing Judy into their secrets, but the likes of Honor, Winn and me were excluded from their world.

Rita Williams was a puzzle. She affected an air of cynicism. Her mother had died four years before, and she had left her father all alone in the old house in Croydon, to join up; but there was a boyfriend, with whom she claimed to have a telepathic link. She came back from course leave married to her Johnnie, and was now Private Bates instead of Private Williams. We were glad for her.

She and I decided one cold day, when the enormous tortoise stove in the hut was greedier than usual, to resort to old sweats' tactics and be resourceful. The sergeants' mess was near our hut, and their coal store nearby. We had to creep along past the cookhouse, under the windows, silently fill the bucket, creep, creep, back again – Aha!

But the third time we made the sortie we were discovered. Such a clatter the cooks made. Bang bang bang on their pans and cans, bang bang bang on their windows. We only realized afterwards that they had waited till we were loaded before chasing us away. So we dared once or twice more. Initiative in the face of the enemy, we called it. Of course!

Rita and I had a fellow feeling: we were the only two who had scraped into kines by standing on tip-toe at the medical/measuring. Sometimes she was an eighth of an inch taller than me: sometimes I was the tall one.

We were punished for a crime, however, soon after the coal-winning exercise. It was not a real, full-scale charge. That would have meant appearing before the commanding officer, having your cap knocked off so that you couldn't salute: the ultimate shame; and being reprimanded or confined to barracks, or worse. No, we hadn't committed any serious crime. We had been late on early morning parade once too often. This made us defaulters, and we were put on defaulters' parade for that evening.

We had seen the daily group of men in disgrace, running round the parade ground, wearing full packs, expiating their sins. The thought of joining them rather annoyed us, and we had all day to think about it. It was a GD officer who had given us the punishment, and it was our officer to whom we appealed to be allowed to do something useful instead of what we had seen. Later a message came to us that we could clean the computing-room windows.

It was not too comfortable, cleaning windows with a regulation gas mask flopping around on your chest, but one of the gunners (probably old Stephen, who had long-service stripes all up his arm) advised us to take out the heavy mask and stuff the haversack with crumpled paper. We began our task with less enthusiasm than we had had before tea but gradually found some satisfaction in it and decided to be late on parade again in about a month's time, when the job would need doing again.

These were the girls I knew best in those early days in the big camp, and we fought and argued and laughed and grumbled and generally got used to the communal life we had to share.

When we found ourselves all thrown together, washing in front of each other, sharing our sleeping-quarters, eating together, working together, suffering our various ailments and female disorders together, sharing our clothes-drying facilities and the iron, we got to know one another pretty well.

Standing at the washbasins one morning, all hastily trying to get as much area washed without exposing too much at a time to the cold, I was the one who answered Verona's question: 'Do you wash hands or face first?' Without thinking, I said, 'Face.' And that started another argument. Balanced on one foot on a duckboard, trying not to get my unoccupied slipper splashed, while my next-door neighbour on the other side was spitting water about in all directions, I was quite relieved when the corporal came to chivvy us, and we could all exchange sympathetic groans.

Washing was uncomfortable. It was not that anyone expected a warmed bathroom in those days (the heat of the water was relied on), but these rows of washbasins were in an exposed row, in a space with doors at both ends. The bath cubicles were quite comfortable, however. No draughts, and a tiny bit of privacy. We kines, after a long, cold day on the large, cold gun-park, used to linger in the bath. The general duties ATS with whom we shared the sanitary block and who had spent their working day in office or store or cookhouse made many a sarcastic remark, and we retaliated until a mutual dislike started to make things a bit uneasy, but the only lasting effect it had was to strengthen our solidarity with one another, and with our own officers.

One notable exception to this animosity was a dear little storewoman we were very fond of. She played the piano: 'Jesu, Joy of Man's Desiring', '*Clair de Lune*' and a Mozart minuet were three of our favourites that she played for us in the rec. hut on barrack nights. She was lively, and a bit of a Mrs Malaprop; she had us laughing all the time. I am sure she did it purposely, to see us laugh. She was a lovely friend to us, giving us the tip whenever something good came into stores, so that by pretending that we had lost a pair of Pantees or collars we could get more, by paying for them.

Clean laundry was returned to us the day before the dirty bundles were collected, if we were lucky. Seven articles could be sent. Our issue was: three pairs of woollen panties (white), three pairs of khaki silk drawers, three vests, three shirts, six collars, three pairs of stockings, two bras, two suspender belts and two towels. Well, work it out. Often a garment would disappear from the communal drying-room, where we put our hand-washed things, and life could get very difficult. 'Lost my shirt in the blizzard, Corporal,' was the best approach.

'Another pair of stockings stolen? Were they marked?'

'Yes, Corporal, but the ink must have faded.'

Well, you have to survive. The basic issue made a daily clean collar just possible, but not a daily shirt, except for the most determined.

The blue-striped flannelette pyjamas were too warm in summer, but in the winter I piled everything on I could find. The stockings were a real nuisance. Nobody in civilian life (except schoolgirls), wore lisle, which was only smoothed-up cotton. They wore out more quickly than silk and had to be darned; their colour faded from one unbecoming colour to a host of other vile ones; they took two days to dry in the summer-time and three or four in the worst of the winter.

All these problems we solved in our own ways, watched one another's behaviour and had bitterly critical things to say about standards other than our own: each of us, of course, was cleaner and more scrupulous than anyone else. But all this had nothing to do with the Army's official obsession with cleanliness, which is mostly concerned with outside appearance. Every detail of behaviour was scrutinized. To smoke, or not? It was the usual thing to smoke cigarettes, and not to was considered unsociable, unfriendly. I hated the taste of tobacco and could never take up the habit. To wear make-up, or not? Several of us were taught how to put on lipstick during that winter and wore make-up for the first time.

And now, with no homework, we had our evenings free. The men we met were mostly on courses at the SAAD, which was Manorbier Camp. We met them during coffee breaks in the NAAFI or the YMCA. The batteries came in usually for about a month, so Honor and I must have met a good many of them in that first winter. They all professed to mix up the two of us: at least, we must be sisters? We couldn't see it, especially Honor, who was taller and more slender than I. We used to look at each other, wondering what the resemblance could be. She was a country girl with a Suffolk accent; I exaggerated my natural Cockney. She had short, curly dark hair and hazel eyes; my mousy hair was long, and my eyes were grey. She had beautiful, long, sweeping eyelashes, but my evenly curved eyebrows were my only beauty. And yet everyone mixed us up.

The food at Manorbier was not particularly good, but it was better than many had found the basic training camp slosh and stodge, so for the duration of the course and for a few weeks after we suffered in comparative silence. But as the weather grew colder and our duties more and more kept us in the open air, we grew hungrier. The food was still being served in the traditional Army 'mess' fashion: four soldiers constituting a mess. Enough for four was put into square mess tins, and we took it in turns to fetch them from the hatch. Meat or fish in one, mash in another, and another vegetable, laughably green, in the third. It was Verona's turn today. We had had a long morning on the gun-park and had to get up there again for the afternoon.

First, the vegetables. Not very appetizing, but food. It was the contents of the third tin that made us rebel. Usually the meat was an unrecognizable brown sludge, which the cook sometimes identified as beef, sometimes mutton; sometimes it came with no name at all. But today's was not sludge. It looked solid. Three very small knobs of something blackish lurked in a greasy gravy. Three.

Verona took the tin back to the hatch, but all the tins had been removed and the orderlies were serving custard and something. No cook: no remedy. Indignation took hold of us.

'Don't let's touch it till the orderly officer comes round.'

'Yes, we'll wait with it all like this. It's time they realized.'

'It looks uneatable, anyway.'

It was one of the unpleasantest of the duty officer's thrice-daily chores to come and ask for any complaints about the food. Usually we had demolished most of it before she turned up, and what could we then say? Uneatable? So this time, starving and knowing that we'd get none of the duff either, we stood our ground.

She came. Bread and cheese were found for us, and nicely stewed apples and custard. What went on behind the scenes we never saw, but the system was changed, as well as the cook.

'And the place is filthy,' we said. 'Couldn't at least the walls be whitewashed, or something?'

'We've no one to do it,' she told us.

'We'll do it,' said Verona. 'We spend a lot of time standing by when the weather is bad.'

'If Miss Clark-Rattray will let us,' someone suggested.

'I'll see what I can do.'

We kines developed over the years a reputation for being able to turn our hand to anything. So now we found ourselves laying the foundation of that reputation. We didn't make a bad job of that cookhouse. Afterwards we had to queue at the hatch, individually; but at least each plate had to have a recognizable amount of food on it. We were hungry, healthy young animals, and we could have eaten anything, within reason.

Most of the washing-up was done by orderlies in the kitchen, but we carried our own 'irons' and mug, washing them at the end of each meal under a cold tap over an open drain gully that was just outside the mess room. The cutlery we shoved into our pockets. It is amazing how quickly you can adjust to conditions. The pint mugs were supplied by some of our best potters: mine was Royal Doulton, bone china – about half an inch thick, and it weighed a ton. Even so, you could see your fingers through it. It was used for tea and cocoa, soup and teeth-cleaning. It was even used for making coal-dust briquettes when we were taught the magic formula: eight parts coal dust, one part cement, one part (or is it two?) water. Mix all in a bucket, and use the mug as a mould.

My parents, too, were learning fast. Their letters were jocularly brave, as always, to save me from worrying. London was not now being bombed, but we girls could all read the signs in letters from home.

Things on the Home Front were changing. The threat of invasion seemed to have passed away, though nothing could be taken for granted, but the sea warfare was worse than ever: things were bad. Wasting food – wasting anything – became tantamount to wasting RN sailors' and merchant seamen's lives. Food rationing became even more severe, and the Robinson Crusoe game in the garden became patriotic as well as self-preserving.

The goat, Binkie, was no more than a pet, and the milk problem was still unsolved. The next attempt at self-sufficiency was more successful, but involved Things That Could Not Be Written Down, and which would have to wait until Christmas for the telling. The net result was a new goat: a broad-in-the-beam adult buff-and-white Toggenburg, with enough milk in her to double their meagre doorstep ration.

My mother had still been reading her library book on the impossibility of amateurs' milking goats when Bessie arrived. And here my delicate nature was spared the details of how one learns to milk and manage a goat, from a book.

5 'Fire!'

Manorbier, Winter 1941–2

We became proficient at our work, and enjoyed it. But it was not all kine work. Sometimes we were wanted on the gun-park, for recording. Every gun and every instrument was fitted with dials and pointers, and our job was to read them and write them down as the gun fired. And, of course, analyze the errors, afterwards.

Recording on the height-finders and predictors was one thing, and a routine job it soon became; but to read the dials on the gun itself was always rather special, and exciting. The noise, the smell of grease and cordite, the shouts, over our shoulders as though we did not exist: we were there in the middle of it, and yet not there.

'Fuze, One oh!'

'Fuze one oh, set!'

The live round heaved up into the breech; the slam shut,

'Ready!'

'FIRE!'

Remember to read the dial.

The shock, and the gun's recoil. The size of it, the nearness of it, the noise of it, the heat of the smoking cartridge case as it shot out of the opened breech and fell to the ground. Watch out! And another round heaved up, ready. It was a grey-green, greasy ballet. The set faces, the shouted orders, the two rows of 'ammunition numbers', moving up one place and taking their turns to feed the gun.

'Fire!' 'Fire!'

But, though we were on the spot, this was not our

dance. We were not part of it. We were just shadows, watching and making notes.

We had to be tested for 'gunshyness'. If you couldn't help blinking when the gun fired, you were no good for this work. And some of us found that it was cumulative. Some could stand it for quite a long time; and suddenly one day it became too much, and one less of our number could be called upon to do it.

A new target was being introduced. Instead of the scarlet cotton sleeve, towed behind a piloted plane, there was an experimental queen bee being developed. It was not always an obedient bee, and swirling flights and whooping flights took place, unnerving all concerned. Naturally it was a very precious object, and gun teams set in a false height or used burst-short ammunition, but on one embarrassing occasion one of the visiting batteries let the side down by actually shooting down the Bee. Hitting the target under any circumstances was so rare that everybody cheered. Val Cox, whose twenty-seventh birthday it was, celebrated by standing on her head – 'to see if I still can'.

However, in spite of the opportunities to meet glamorous characters on the gun-park, most of us preferred manning our kine 'A' or 'B' station. It was a taste of independent life. Out there on the cliff, it was like a little house. In spite of the drill book, and as well as the official list of equipment to be taken out, the most important gear was stuff to light the fire, something to heat water in and a frying-pan. And some provisions.

While the weather was good, we became more confident in the work and were content to catch up with letter-writing when it rained. But it was the Welsh mist that teased. Everything would be set out, and down it would come, leaving us all 'standing by'. How we came to hate the very word!

Boring jobs were found for us to do. Gunnery drill was always being changed: the very work we were doing was changing some of it. So the drill books had to be kept up-to-date. Amendments. Scissors and gum. The gum of those days! Nasty, dribbly stuff that stretched the paper.

'For "home" substitute "flush with the bases of the

cartridge cases".' Cut it out from the amendment sheet, stick it in place, if there is room. It was a boring detail, intricate and fiddly. There was one that amused us: 'The GPO [that is, the gun position officer] shouts "STOP!" The detachment continues its duties.'

'Stooges! That's all we are. Stooges!' said Honor, after one particularly frustrating day.

As the winter progressed, our trivial discomforts increased. The weather was always wet and windy or damp. It was never frosty, but the chill bit. Mice began to seek our warmth in the hut, and we had one who used to be among the ashes of the hearth in the mornings. Honor and the mouse used to regard each other without moving, and she kindly hypnotized him for us while the rest of us got dressed. But one day he disappeared.

'Has anybody seen my mouse?'

Why this should have made us laugh, goodness knows, but we all found it very funny.

Worse was to come later. It was colder and windy, the electric lines blew down, and the huts were in darkness. Candles were brought to us, and that was when we discovered that it was useless to put your candle near the joining of two planks of the wall. It would simply blow out.

The mouse did not return, and soon the droppings we were sweeping up in the mornings were bigger than the mouse's.

Our report to Authority was rebuffed. Imagination, they said. So we suffered anxiously a night or two more, expecting to be devoured in our beds. Then, in the middle of one night, Rita Bates shrieked, leapt out of bed and put on the light.

'Put that light out!'

'Put up the blackout!'

'That,' she announced firmly, 'was a rat.'

And, shuddering as she was with shock, she bravely stripped the bed and pulled up the sheet. And, sure enough, there were dirty scratches and tears. We all searched for the rest of the night, not daring to put out the light again, but found nothing.

First thing in the morning, she and I went down to confront the duty officer. It happened to be Clark-Rattray, and we were sorry that it was she who received our dramatic gesture, but we had rehearsed it, and the sweeping of the filthy evidence across her desk seemed to save a lot of words. She was very upset, and an hour later 'rat sandwiches' were prepared, and after that we each slept with one under the bed.

It was a pity: we would so like it to have been a GD (general duties) officer on duty that day. The majority of ATS officers, who performed the ordinary duties of discipline and administration, seemed to us to have been chosen as the Royal Navy was famous for choosing: not so much what you can do, as who you are. Men born into good families are 'born to command', as they used to say; but this did not necessarily apply to their sisters, and a mixed bunch we found the general duties officers.

On the other hand, we respected our own officers, because we respected ability. Women had to combat many prejudices from men, many of whom resented our presence in the forces, particularly if we were employed not only as clearers-up or other menials. The lower the rank, we found, the more difficult they found it to accept us. The male officers we worked with were mostly the scientific and technical brains, inventing the ideas which we worked out. We could have swallowed more kindly their lack of regard for us than that of other women. Apart from our own kine officers, whose dominion over us we accepted by and large, because we recognized the skills they had, the female officers we had contact with were Administration. They were responsible for feeding, clothing, housing and paying us. They inspected and disciplined us, and for all these things we were disrespectfully ungrateful. In our minds we lumped them all together as 'general duties' officers. It was not a term they would have used themselves.

We thought it was a pity, and a wasted opportunity, that the rat had chosen that particular night.

The weather grew more unkind, and the ATS Higher Command had been demanding more suitable dress for us on duty. The cliff-top gun-park was about as breezy a place as could be imagined, and our knee-length skirts were not much protection. At last, permission was given and a battledress was put into production. Boots were also asked for. And, such is the Army's way, as soon as permission was granted, we were to be allowed to wear such battledress as was available. From the men's store, of course.

'Fall in! By the left, quick march!'

The general duties corporal took us down to the store. All ATS were regarded with some jocularity by the men, and this morning's duty they seemed to find very amusing.

'What's your breech measurement?'

'Let me measure your chest!'

We sorted out what we could, and staggered out with armfuls of what felt like sandpaper.

Verona was the first into her outfit. At five feet eleven tall, and slender, she looked almost stylish. They had given us braces, because no one had sanctioned belts. We were not complaining: none of us wanted to add blancoing belts to the rest of our chores.

I couldn't manage mine at all. Eventually they all had a go at helping me. My size and shape and the immense length of what I had been given somehow were just not compatible. And soldier's khaki, when brand new, is of incredible stiffness, bristly as a pot-scourer and of monstrous weight.

Well, here we go, Trousers first. One foot in – lose balance – all fall down – legs up in the air – put the other foot in – feet lost half way – pull hard – still no feet – surrounded by helpless mirth – shut up, you idiots – if I stop to giggle, I'll lose myself entirely. Pull again – how much further? There's one foot, and there's some toes.

'Do them up, then,' they shrieked. Wriggle, wriggle. Fly buttons. How unladylike. Metal buttons into rock-hard, brand-new buttonholes is difficult and undignified. There was a cotton label stitched on the bottom, on the right buttock: 'Height six foot two; breech 38.' I managed to pull the last eighteen inches or so of unoccupied trouser legs up over my feet and stood up in my hairy concertinas, girded up to the armpits.

'Don't forget the braces!'

Well, there I stood, W/76779 Brewer D., complete with

blue shoulder-straps. It was nice and warm, anyhow. And, pausing to be serious, I could cut a foot or so off the legs and manage somehow.

The others had, by now, also struggled into their finery. Now for the battletops. No buttons to polish, at least. There were khaki loops and brass bits dangling about, for the webbing that luckily we had not got. Verona pulled the whole contraption up over my ears and stuck my cap on top, declaring it a great improvement. Just then the stony-faced corporal appeared in the doorway. We watched her carefully, but her face did not move.

'They're only lent. You're not to cut them or mutilate them in any way. They're to go back to stores as soon as ATS issue arrives.'

There were no boots yet, of course. We continued to use our ordinary shoes.

For the next two months I paraded and spent my working days with trouser legs down to the ankle, turned up as far as the knees and down to the ankle again; and a battletop that everyone agreed looked like Dog Toby's frill. And yet – and yet, there was a thrill in it. We were doing a man's job, in man's attire. This is what we had joined for. On the day the ATS battledress arrived, we were almost sorry to give back our unbecoming plumes.

The new slacks (women did not wear skin-tight pants in those days; it would have been considered indecent) were of fine serge, soft to the touch compared with what we had been wearing, with a decorous side opening fastened with two visible buttons, and almost flattering to some of our shapes. Winn, for one, was pleased with the change. Her delicate spirit had not liked the masquerade. We felt almost female again. But it was not so warm as the other! Later, much later, we were given leather jerkins also. Of all the garments a soldier can be issued with, this, surely, must be the best loved. Soft, thick leather, lined with khaki flannel and buttoned front. It was completely windproof.

And so, chinstraps down and battledressed, we survived our first Manorbier winter.

The revelation of our variously green cotton legs was reserved for the evenings, when we wished to look entrancing. Aesthetics as well as modesty kept our underwear firmly hidden. 'Passion-killers', as the most reticent of us called them, were rather a problem. The skirt had been raised an inch or so, to keep up with economical war-time fashions, but the underwear was not altered. In the early days the khaki directoire knickers were of pure Celanese silk. They came in three sizes: large, enormous and elephantine. Rita and I had occasion to be issued with new ones on the same day once, and unfortunately the stores had only size 3 for us. Back in the hut, we modelled our acquisitions, leaping from bed to bed. No one guessed that we had our skirts on underneath.

Val told us the pathetic tale of her experience at the gate of Talavera Camp, Northampton, one night. She had returned to barracks after an evening in the town, and just as the sentry said, 'Advance, friend, to be recognized,' her waist elastic broke, and down slithered the Garments, as only silk can slither. But the knee elastics stood firm ...

We kines were very proud to wear the gun of the Royal Artillery as our special badge above the left breast pocket. The other ATS ack-ack artillery girls, of the mixed batteries, which actually engaged the enemy during real air raids, wore the flaring bomb, as worn by the fusilier regiments, and we counted ourselves fortunate to have the cannon as our emblem. On the service dress tunic that we wore with a skirt, the badge was a brass one, to go with the brass buttons. But more suitable for battledress was the embroidered equivalent, which had to be sewn on. We had all very carefully used buttonhole stitches and thought the effect very elegant.

Equally pleasing was being required to wear the white lanyard of the Royal Artillery. The story had been told us: the legend of the gun that could not be fired safely during a famous battle, for want of a lanyard; of the extreme heroism that kept the gun firing, anyway, and the rather complicated tradition that led to a lanyard's being worn by every single member of the regiment; and that other tradition whereby the RA always parades in the place of honour on the right of the line, on ceremonial occasions. So the lanyard – a white lanyard, against all reason and usefulness – is worn on the right shoulder as a compliment.

The RA's cap badge, which of course we did not wear, carries their motto, 'Where Right and Glory Lead', and their one battle honour.

Every regiment, on its badge and on its colours, carries the names of battles at which they have distinguished themselves. The Royal Artillery carries no place-names: it simply says *'Ubique'* – 'Everywhere'. We were very conscious of the honour of wearing their emblem.

There was a buzz in the camp. Royalty was coming to visit us. Her Royal Highness Princess Mary, the Princess Royal, our patron and commanding officer, was coming to Manorbier.

We practised our marching, fast and slow, our saluting, our standing still and our falling in and out. We practised facing this way and that. 'Open order – march!' Open order and close order, all over the parade ground, in little squads, according to our units.

On the day before The Day, we were all combined into one parade. This was where the general duties officer, the ATS camp commandant, pulled her rank. She wore a crown on her shoulder, while our highest rank was three pips.

The battle of wits began.

The first thing that happened was that we were all paraded in one long line, all the length of the ground.

'From the right – tallest on the right – shortest on the left – size!'

Consternation on our part. To be all mixed up, and separated from one's unit. Then chaos, and some sort of shambling attempt. I worked my depressing way down to the left, further and further away from my tall colleagues. Rita was also approaching the low end, too, but we completely lost sight of all the others.

Then the boring succession of inspections began, by ever-ascending ranks. First a corporal, who brought us up to stiffer attention and left us at ease, till someone came out of the orderly room and stood us easy.

Then a sergeant came, with a few caustic things to say. Five minutes' wait.

The CSM. A more detailed scrutiny, this time. Then a

young officer passed hastily along – and rapidly retreated.

A junior commander whom we did not know could be heard, pecking away at small details. Her high-pitched voice carried, stridently criticizing angle of cap, angle of toes.

And then, at last, Madam: Senior Commander, ATS, Western Command. She squinted and poked, trying to find the tiniest fault, and at last she trapped a smile behind her teeth.

'Junior Commander!' The unfortunate kine officer came forward to be criticized. 'Tell these auxiliaries to take off those extraneous fal-lals. They make the parade look very untidy.'

'Kine personnel – one pace forward – march!' We all stood forth. 'Lanyards, remove. Put them in your pockets. Brass guns, remove. Put them in your pockets.' We did so, burning, with nothing but two raw holes where the split pins had gone through.

'One pace backward – march! Pick up your dressing.'

When the practice parade was over, we glowered our way back to our hut. What was to be done? We wouldn't take this lying down.

We sat on our beds, fuming. Rita strode up and down, jerking out her hands angrily, smoking furiously, muttering.

'Let's send a message,' Winn suggested. 'They maybe don't know how much it means to us.'

Molly, Val and Verona rounded on her.

'Oh, yes, they do. I bet that's why she did it.'

'They don't like us.'

'They'll never listen to us. Besides, there isn't time. The parade's tomorrow. You know what the Army's like. Every decision takes about ten years.'

'I'm putting mine on again.'

'What's the use of that, Doffy? They'll only order us to strip them off again.'

'Pity it's not battledress parade. You can't take unpicking scissors on to the parade ground.'

We agonized and fretted, and the idea came to us all at once. We spent an hour, unpicking our fabric guns off the battle-blouses and neatly, and strongly, sewing them onto the service tunics. After a long discussion, we decided to put on the lanyards as well. They might be ordered off us, but at least we'd have made the gesture. We were all defiance. No message came from the kine office, and we went to sleep that night ready for the Battle of Manorbier.

The visit of the princess was scheduled for twelve noon, so naturally in good Army fashion we were paraded at nine o'clock.

'Get fell in!'

The long line of mixed ATS formed again, as yesterday. We were stood at ease, then easy.

A sergeant came to get us into the square formation that we had rehearsed the day before, and after about half-an-hour we were almost in position.

Another sergeant came and shifted us about a bit.

A few more minutes passed, then a subaltern came out, took over from the sergeant and began giving a few practice orders. Nobody seemed to have noticed our rebellion.

Then a junior commander came: another one this time. She took one startled glance and disappeared again.

Minutes passed.

Then, Madam, looking splendid, came out.

And here, we must give her full marks. She, quite serene, looked upon us almost gently.

'I have decided,' she announced in a stage bellow, to her subordinate, 'that the weather is somewhat inclement. All auxiliaries will return to quarters and redeploy in ten minutes' time. In greatcoats.' And she eyed each one of us in turn, slowly working from left to right, then squarely strode off. 'Carry on, Sergeant.'

Greatcoats! No distinguishing badges or accoutrements are worn on great coats. Badges of rank only. The crafty old –! We thought of more synonyms for senior ATS officers than we had ever concentrated before. But you had to hand it to her. To come up with that, in a matter of moments! We almost laughed.

The anonymous greatcoat! Covering all!

By noon we were almost cheerful and were glad to see our princess. She came and looked at us; she spoke to some, then disappeared into the officers' mess. And later she came to look at the kines.

But our war with GD officers had locked on.

We solemnly licked a finger, however, chalked one up in the sky to her, this time. Officialdom had won this round.

Almost immediately after Christmas leave, while the girls were still laughing about the goat and at the photos of me as a bridesmaid, in my pinky slinky princess dress ('Coo!' a bystander had remarked, 'Ain't she go' a pre'y figure? She goes in an'aht like a peanut!'), word came that my mother was ill.

She had to have a hysterectomy. She did not use that word in her letter: she gave me no details at all, just that she was going to have an operation. But her sister, the single one, who was a nurse, wrote to tell me what it was. It was one of those things that no one spoke of in those days. Women whispered about 'having their womb taken away', making sure that no child or man was in earshot. It was an operation undertaken only in extreme need. My mother had suffered the effects of a bad prolapse ever since my birth, and no operation had been suggested to her before.

So this meant something else. The unspoken danger: the then unspeakable word.

That night, on compassionate leave, I was on a troop train. To be the only girl on a train full of men caused me no concern now, and I had other things to worry about. The carriages were full; even the luggage racks each had a soldier stretched out, ready for his night's repose. The only hope of a reasonable journey was in the corridor. The train was packed with bodies, everyone trussed into greatcoats and, this being a posting for the men, they were strapped around by webbing and had their full kit with them. There was hardly any light: what lamps there were had slitted masks across them. With that easy philosophy of the soldier, if the beer is all drunk and there is not enough light to see the cards, everyone settles down to sleep. Dark and cold, the train stuffy from its last occupants, it promised to be an unpleasant night. But a kitbag or two (and there were plenty to borrow) make quite a comfortable bed.

The journey began at eight o'clock in the evening, and with any luck we should arrive in London at about four in the morning.

'Hullo, Smiler!' Someone had addressed me. I peered into the murk and saw that it was 'Tiny', an enormous Canadian whom I remembered from the gun-park and who was trying to get his huge frame settled into the corner of the corridor.

'Come here, little Miss,' he invited me; and thus befriended I eventually dozed off.

It must have been hours later that I stirred, feeling something pressing on my ears. It was Tiny's great hands.

'It's all right. Go to sleep again. You don't want to hear what they're talking about. Go to sleep. That's the best thing for you.'

And so I was guarded from the dangers of the night. Dear Tiny! I wonder if he ever realized how grateful I was to him.

All this does not seem very long ago to me, but fifty years is a long time, and many things change in half a century.

The world of medicine might have been another planet. It was the world before penicillin, before antibiotics, before the lovely painless white antiseptic creams, before May & Baker had developed their miracle cure for pneumonia. Infectious fevers were still dread scourges.

It was the world of biting iodine, where carbolic was the only disinfectant. Hospitals stank of it, and drains were scrubbed with Condy's Fluid, made by dissolving purple permanganate of potash, which stained everything indelibly dark brown.

And medical care was expensive. The National Health Service was not universal: it was only for industrial workers and their wives, and it covered GPs' fees and some medicines, but only part of hospital fees. Many people never went near a doctor all their lives. They called in the 'trained nurse', who usually lived nearby, or the local midwife. Or they went to the chemist, who would recommend or make up something.

Of course, every parish had accommodation for the very poor who were sick. The old workhouses were still standing, and two wards were reserved for the homeless and the destitute; many poor people had no choice but to end their days in these old infirmaries.

But we were lucky: this was a teaching hospital.

The porter consulted his list that hung in full view from the window. I did not have to plead: only child, on leave. He did not phone the ward, just said, 'Right-oh. You can go straight in.'

My heart turned cold. She was on the list. The danger list. 'On the gate,' Daddy muttered as we went in.

'She's over there,' whispered the woman in the first bed. 'She's been waiting for you. What's that you've got? Eggs? Put her name on them, then they can't pretend to mix them up. You'd be surprised what goes on in here.'

It was customary to take food in to patients. It had nothing to do with wartime shortages. Hospitals were privately run, even this one, and mostly funded by charities.

The ward was dark and smelt acrid, like all hospital wards. She was already being sedated for the operation. It was dark, like a vault. Sandbags were stacked outside, against the tall windows, only a tiny slit of light and air left at the top of each one. The feeble light showed the twelve beds, all occupied.

'They're all fifty-three, same as me,' whispered my mother. 'It must be some sort of experiment.' She looked very tired and thin. 'It's only a little operation. It's something I should have had done years ago. It's quite common now. Everybody's having it done.'

We must have said something to her, but she had to talk. Trying so hard not to say, 'Don't worry.'

'That woman over there. Her only daughter was killed in an air raid. And see that one? The one with the hyacinths? She's had so much trouble, poor thing. Her husband left her, and her boys are still at school. So many people, and so many troubles.' And she hugged me with what strength she had, and kept hold of my father's hand. 'Now, you mustn't come back till six o'clock. They won't let you in, if you do. Off you go. I'll be all right. I promise you. God is with me. And remember – All things work together for good, to them that love God.'

She was always like that. We had come to try to cheer her

up, but who was doing the cheering?

Another woman called us over and told us: 'She's very ill. But she's got a good chance. She's brave enough for all of us.'

This was the first time I had felt really frightened. Faith. One must have faith. Daddy and I walked out in a daze. The chickens had to be fed, the goats and the rabbits. And Bessie had to be milked. We turned into the market-place, and instead of going in to Cramphorn's, the corn chandler's, we crossed the road without a word and together in unison and in step walked into the church. We knelt down together. Nothing was said aloud. And afterwards, ever afterwards, it was never mentioned between us.

After the longest afternoon of our lives, we went to the gate again. She had come through.

The next few days, we dared to believe that she would be well again one day. Now all that was needed was time to heal. There were no aids to healing: only good health, cleanliness and good food. Healthy flesh would heal, given time. Time.

'Stay in bed for a month, and you are to do nothing' – the surgeon – 'Nothing, do you understand?' – looking fiercely at my father 'for two years. Spend all day with your feet up. Take up knitting or something.'

She was the eldest of eight brothers and sisters. The five married ones all offered to take her and look after her. She was to go to Golders Green for a month or so, and then to High Wycombe, to her youngest sister.

I went back to Manorbier, leaving her with her brother and his family, and my Dad with all the animals.

Thank God there were no air raids.

Back to camp. The few days away had felt like a long time, and it was difficult to settle again, but there was little time to mope. From seven in the morning until 10.30 at night, life consisted of a thousand small organized incidents and duties, crowding each minute.

The first hasty wash, then scrambling into clothes, hurrying across the camp to morning parade, into the mess, back to the hut to clean kit and tidy up, out onto the gun-park, and after canteen break, back on duty, into the mess again, back and forth and here and there from early dark to dusk.

Or it might be out to stations. The kine instruments were permanently on their pedestals, protected by a roof-sliding hut. Here, life was our own. Out on the cliffs the heart could lift and the soul breathe. The tempo was different. Only Nature surrounded the small square hut. Sky, sea, wind, rocks, scrub and turf; white birds screaming and Caldy Island like a benevolent spirit on the horizon.

In the hut was a small iron stove with a tin chimney. Just the thing for brewing up. You can tell an ex-kine by the speed with which she can get a pot boiling, starting with a cold, obstinate stove, a few sticks and a bit of flammable celluloid film, while at the same time setting up a field telephone. Honor was our best fire-lighter, closely followed by Winn, who in her quiet way joined in with everything and kept us supplied with hot drinks, purring over us as if we were her kittens. Woe, of course, betide any no.3 who got through to CC Post, acknowledging that we were ready for action, before the fire was well alight.

On Sundays we were free. We liked to go to Manorbier village for morning prayer. The vicar was the camp padre, but we preferred to attend his ancient church, which stands high above the bay, facing the castle – Gerald Cambriensis's castle – which dominates the right-hand height. It is a spectacular setting, and it suited the mood of the times.

We sang: 'God of our fathers, unto Thee/Our fathers cried in danger's hour,' and 'Once to every man and nation/Comes the moment to decide ...' and 'Holy Father, in Thy mercy/Hear our anxious prayer:/Keep our loved ones, now far absent,/'Neath Thy care.' We sang the *Venite* with fervour and the *Te Deum* in faith, believing in the peace of Christ, and hearing from our gentle friend the gospel of love, confirming our faith in Christ's sacrifice, His goodness, and accepting His grace, in trust. Crimond, and 'Eternal Father', holding back the tears; and we spent the rest of the day behind our smokescreen of frivolous conversation.

We liked to walk. Some, like me, had to *learn* to walk in the country. 'No civilized pavements!' I grumbled one day, causing much mirth.

One day we discovered the watercress that grows in the stream that bubbles up a hundred yards from Manorbier beach and spreads itself, making a delta in the soft sand. The spring bubbles cool and clear, and there grow what certainly resembled cresses. But this was not the shiny, round-leafed variety that is sold in London: this was paler and had oblong leaves.

'Oh, you!' said Honor. 'If it's not tied up with string, with "2d" marked round its neck, you don't think it's real.'

Near the castle, on a grassy rise, stood the 'Dak' bungalow, where 'Mrs Dak' could always produce a nicely poached egg on toast, sending her husband out to perambulate the place in his linen suit and panama hat, summer or winter, while she was busy.

We rejoiced in the early spring. Snowdrops grew everywhere; herb robert and cuckoo-pint appeared incredibly early, and ferns of all kinds grew out of the red sandstone. Primroses a foot high popped their sweet heads above the banks of the little streams.

It was on the last day of February, a delightfully mild day, that we took our first swim of the season. We must have been idiots. The water was cold: too cold. But we discovered a technique that worked. You paddled till your feel were numb, then took the plunge. It was – just – bearable. And it didn't kill any of us.

All too soon, it was Monday again, when all day long the bugle chased us: waking us up, calling us to eat, sending us out on parade; and in the evening, calling flags to be lowered and lamps lit, the guard to take post and calling us home.

Another turn had taken place in the war. Now that America and Japan had taken up arms, all the world that mattered was involved.

Posters appeared everywhere: 'Careless Talk Costs Lives.' A wall with a great ear sticking out, or a bearded spy under a candle-lit tête-a-tête table. 'Be like Dad. Keep Mum.' (What a furore that one caused!)

'Doffy' Brewer
(France and
Germany star given
to the Breda girls for
April–May 1945)

Teaching – a blitz-
free Saturday. Six of
my girls at Kew
Gardens, May 1941

How to test the
accuracy of
gunfire

Develop and dry
the film – lots of
meths for speed
– Sheila Caws
scrutinizing

Evaluate and
tabulate – Joan
Thirlwall and
Kath Davies

After computing,
draw up the
results – Kathleen
Lavery

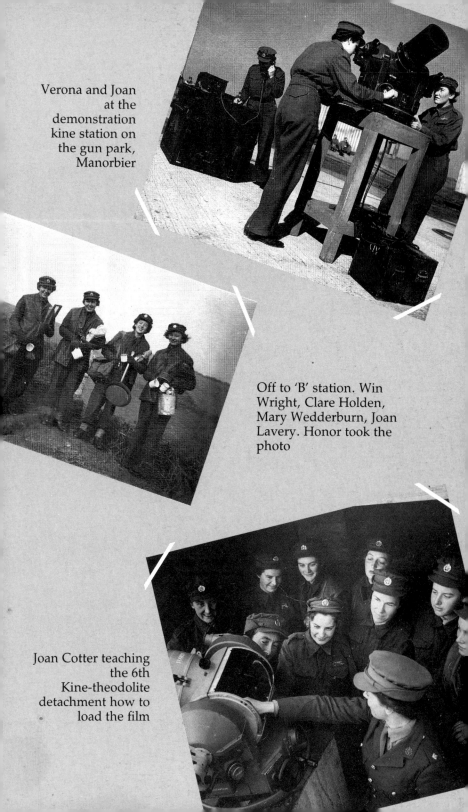

Verona and Joan at the demonstration kine station on the gun park, Manorbier

Off to 'B' station. Win Wright, Clare Holden, Mary Wedderburn, Joan Lavery. Honor took the photo

Joan Cotter teaching the 6th Kine-theodolite detachment how to load the film

Our main reference point at Lydstep:
Caldey Lighthouse

Christmas Day, 1942: Honor and I at either end
and Bing sitting in front

Rita Bates on the
rocks at Lydstep

Weekend Lydsteppers, including Heather Geary (third from left, front), top man Val Cox and service-dressed Molly Tapp

Joan Lavery, with field telephone and head-and-breast set

Outside Mrs Walters's shop at Lydstep. Between Winn and Mary Cowan, Margaret ('Scottie') Scott

Sue Turnpenny, pouring a drink for Joy Dalby

Our boarding-house at Clacton. From right to left: Peg Adams, Kay Parry, Pat Wadia; Betty, Isabel and Olive; Val Cox, Joan Moss *et al*

THE CROFT

Gun-park gear: battledress, leather jerkin, gloves

No kines at Clacton – just an old Vickers predictor! Betty Goodfellow and Winn Goldson

Recording the V2's flight in Germany, later on.
We spent months in 1944–45 trying to locate
the launch sites of the V2 all the way from
Walcheren to the Hague – not knowing that
they could be run on this (above)!

We went to Breda, Holland, at the beginning of April 1945 and photographed the 'Card Sharp' and ourselves in jocular mood. Flea, Joy and Verna; me, Ann and Gladys; Sue, Norah, Verona, Ruby.

Canteen conversation became dafter and dafter. All the gossip; and the usual apocryphal stories about incompetent officers, the Gunner Who Disappeared and, of course, the daft rookie. A sentry was supposed to have been on guard, up in the field on the Manorbier side of the camp. His officer, anxious that he was all right, went along to see how he was getting on. He found him staring into the dark; but the sentry, who recognized his own officer when he was near enough to disarm him, said nothing. The officer, trying to be helpful and not wanting to put him on a charge, prompted him. 'Halt – who goes there?' he suggested. 'Friend!' replied the sentry.

Honor and I, being of a practical disposition, said, 'What field?' Then everyone went quiet and changed the subject. But soon after that, Honor wangled an invitation for the two of us to visit whatever was being guarded. We should have to be careful. The GL operator said that tonight's sentry was a friend of his and would let us through. Would we care to see the latest miracle of science?

We felt very daring, but it was too good to miss. It was a cold evening, not raining, but the grass was damp. We crept along and gradually could discern the tall, square box that contained the mysteries. We knocked gently on the door, which promptly opened. Our friend got us inside quickly and shut the door. It was a very small space, but the bench was just big enough for the three of us to squeeze in. In front of us, not two feet away from our noses, was the Tube, a cathode-ray tube. A blue-green line trembled across its face, and by its dim light we could just see the control knobs below it.

'There's my little treasure,' he said. 'What do you think of her?'

'Tell us,' we implored him, 'Tell us what it does.'

The line wavered and twinkled, and suddenly a blip shot up and disappeared.

'There!' he whispered. 'That's it.'

'That's it?' We thought of the risks we had run to come here.

'Look!' The blip reappeared and he twiddled one or two of his dials. He played a little game with it, and the loop lengthened, then shot up again and finally settled.

'That's an aircraft. Would you like to know how far away it is? This' – indicating his dancing line – 'this is the base, and that represents the distance. It's time, really. But it amounts to the same thing. You know – radio waves – light waves – constant speed. So that's the time base. Reading from the left. Any metal object reflects it, and the message is received along the base. All you've got to do is divide by two, and you've got the range.'

He let us work out for ourselves why it had to be divided by two, while he adjusted something else, and I thought of the television set that a friend of mine had, at home. It was always playing up. Every time a car went by, every time a plane went over. Interference. Oh! But he was talking again.

'It gives direction and range. All at once. No messing about. Just read it off the dial.' And, beaming at us in the eerie blue light, like an eager teacher, encouraging his charges to think, 'What's the most important thing of all?' We were still bemused. 'It works in the dark. That's the thing. It can see in the dark.'

It was breathtaking. Even we could see that it was going to revolutionize everything. I thought of the London gun teams, with their slow searchlights, banging away at the spaces between the bombers, however thick they seemed.

'At last you'll have an instant present position to work from.'

We tiptoed back to the hut in great excitement. We had shared in history-making.

Rumours had begun to percolate through the coffee-times that our detachment was heading for something special. A new establishment was being talked of, Trials Wing, and it looked as though some of us might be chosen for it. Already, we knew, some hand-picked kines had gone to Aberporth, where important things were happening. And now?

The set that Honor and I had seen was called a 'GL' (gun-laying) receiver. Its transmitter, which we could now identify in daylight, was in a corner of the field and was called Elsie – SLC. The system was called radiolocation. The word 'radar' had never been heard by the likes of us. Perhaps, even, it had not yet been coined.

6 ' "I see," said the Blind Man'

Lydstep, Spring 1942

Of all the places to which we could have been posted, Lydstep is what stays in the memory and in the heart. Nothing could have been more different from the atmosphere of the large, open military camp that was Manorbier, with its grey, square buildings, its guardroom, parade-ground, wind-swept gun-park, squads of gunners hither and thither at the double, officers to be saluted every ten yards along the clinically clean roads and paths, with their whitewashed boulders at every corner, and the bugle calls.

All we knew of our new home was the café at the top of a small lane. The lane was guarded by sentries who were quartered in a pleasant house on the other corner from the café. The road to Tenby continued from that point in a great curve above the mile-long bay, where South Lodge indicated the other end of the estate and was similarly guarded. It was a little secret world. Only the tops of trees could be seen from the road, and the sea beyond, and Caldy Island.

We were to work in Lydstep House, which was situated down near the beach at the western end of the bay, at the foot of the little lane that had been forbidden to us. Now we were allowed to pass the sentry and go down the steep track. A high hedge on the left, and a more accessible field on the right. Halfway down to the sea, the lane took a sharp turn to the left, and on the angle, facing us as we approached, a small bungalow.

Only twelve of us were the pioneers: the facilities, it was explained to us, could not support the whole detachment.

We had a look round our new home. A real little house! One room was to be our rec. room, another our mess, and the kitchen was a real, old-fashioned country kitchen with a quarry-tiled floor and the old coal-fired range in the corner. One of the orderlies had preceded us, and tea was being prepared. (The Army method of making tea is standard: two buckets of water are put on to boil, then into each go a quarter of tea and a tin of evaporated milk; a pound of sugar is put into one bucket, and tea is ready. 'With or Without?')

The hut that we were to sleep in was a Nissen. There were two, one behind the other, on what had been a lawn. Very different from the vast Mae West hut. This looked, at first glance, almost cosy. Room for only twelve beds, with not much space between them, a small black stove in the middle, with 'pokers, soldiers, one' and 'shovels, officers, one' at the ready. (That was a kindness on someone's part – 'shovels soldier' had rough handles and wobbly edges; 'shovels, officer' were smooth and were a good, quick dustpan.) The floor was concrete; the only windows (non-openable) were at the two ends of the hut, so a door would have to be left open for ventilation. Never mind – our first concern was to bag a bed.

The 6th KT had been made up to strength by a recent course, and we had some of them now with us. Honor, Winn and I took the first three beds on the right. Opposite us were Beth Sagar, Kathleen Lavery and Kathleen Davies. Next to Kath was Rita, then Heather Geary and Win Wright; opposite them were Verona, Lois Howes and Margaret Scott. Frosty was to sleep in the bungalow with our new sergeant, who would follow with the rest later; and our officer, Marnette Linton, was to be quartered down in the house, with the Trials Wing officers and administration.

We soon discovered the lack of 'facilities'. A sanitary block was being built on the veranda of the bungalow, but it was not finished. In the meantime, we shared the single loo; each of us was given a small galvanized iron basin and shown where the rain-water butt was; we'd have to walk over to top camp for a bath. But it was 1 May, we were young and healthy, the weather was kind for these first few days, and we had been chosen for special work of some sort. So we set our washbasins on the low brick wall, splashed around a bit and took it all in good spirits.

The very smell of the place was different from the camp: it smelt of vegetation. The twelve of us tried to march down the steeper, stony lane to the beach, but our shoes did not like the jagged stones that had made the hasty roadway. Those of us on the left were thankful to walk on the green edge, sliding a little on the fleshy plants. They were rather like bluebells but were white, their bells making a crown. Very pretty.

But whatever was that horrible smell?

Verona's voice was the first to be heard, as we crushed the delicate blossoms: 'Pooh! Ich! Yuk! Whatever's that smell?'

Of course – wild garlic! It was a smell, and taste, we were not used to, in those days, and it was quite a shock.

But the whole place was so green, and we could hear the sea now, dragging on the shingle, and there were the roofs of Lydstep House, beyond the trees. To the right of us, high above, towered the headland, where all the secret equipment was, and as we grumbled and found fault with all the silly details, our hearts sang with excitement.

But first, breakfast. We were to mess with the men until such time as the rest of the the detachment could be accommodated and our own cook arrived. As we entered the Nissen hut that had been erected on the pebble beach, we were greeted with loud cheers. These men were the permanent staff, who included men who were medically graded C3 (unfit for the fighting line) and who spent their time humping instruments and guns about, guarding them, keeping stores, manning the orderly room and taking messages, including mail. They looked unlikely as beaux; but they welcomed us and had saved us two tables near the door. We soon saw why. Every time we went to where the breakfast was, we had to file past them all. 'Whew, whew!' Well, we had to take it as a compliment. What else could you do?

The sound and smell of the sea, the quantities of porridge and fried bread and tea improved our tempers still more, and by the time we reported for duty, we had forgotten to grumble at anything.

The house was an Edwardian copy of a Tudor mansion. Heavily timbered, amply proportioned, it was a delightful, real house. The oak staircase was worth going in to see. Our computing-room was the library. The books had all been taken away, and the only furniture was the usual set of six-foot tables and wooden forms, but there was a great open fireplace, a minstrels' gallery and a large window looking onto the garden, which was really the beginning of the wood. Winn and I, who worked together, bagged a strategic place near the fireplace but also near a small side window. It was line-of-sight with the door, which later was to prove useful.

That day we met Major 'Mac' McMullen. We had only seen him as the presiding genius on the big gun-park and had overheard a terse comment or two sometimes. He had the reputation of being a stickler. Anyone working for him had to work. He was a familiar figure to us, out-of-doors, wearing a Glengarry cap instead of the usual Army cap with the red band which was the mark of an IG (instructor of gunnery). Warrant officers, assistant instructors of gunnery, wore a white band. At close quarters he looked smaller, but dynamic. He seemed to radiate energy. Small bright eyes, a hooked nose and a mouth full of amusement: woe betide anyone against whom that wryness was directed!

He briefly welcomed us to Trials Wing and told us that our brief was to 'improve the performance of the AA batteries' and that the work would take several forms: to devise better drills for the existing fire-control methods, to improve those methods and – most important and, he ventured to say, the most exciting – to adapt radiolocation methods for use directly with the guns: light and heavy.

'By the way,' he said, 'we shall now use the word "radar" for all radiolocation, GL, or whatever you have heard it called before.'

We should be working at stations with the kine, recording on the radar instruments on the headland here, recording on the big gun-park at Manorbier for experimental shoots, as well as computing and analyzing results for War Office reports, here in the library.

'Oh – and some of you may find yourselves working with Major Harding. He's the boffin, a wizard with radio waves. He's full of ideas, and if you want to work for him, you'll have to be quick.'

We had, of course, heard of George Harding and occasionally had heard his voice on the other side of a hardboard partition in the computing-hut at Manorbier. He affected an exaggerated drawl, and his voice rose and swooped in a manner that made us hysterical. To be working for him! Some of our favourite giggles were over something that George was supposed to have said.

So here were our two IGs. And we, who had had a bath in a pudding basin, were going to spend our working days in a mansion in an artificial wood in our own private bay. The very loo was palatial: all that polished wood and fancy tiling, a large mirror and an ante-room with a washbasin you could have curled up in. There was a NAAFI, further along the beach, and altogether we thought it was not too bad.

Memory has melted the first week or two into one long sunny day: our routine settled down very quickly, and we soon adapted to the work and became more familiar with one another.

There was a natural tendency to have one 'special' friend or to be one of a threesome, but we were very flexible and were not too exclusive in our friendships. Saturday morning in the hut was the time for arguments. Half-day working, and the possibility of catching the bus to Tenby in the afternoon. Honor, Winn and I would be deciding whether to go to the dance in the evening or to the cinema. Win and Heather made us all ashamed: where Honor and I tried to convince each other, and Winn, to our own point of view, Heather and Win Wright would be saying, 'But I'm sure you'd rather go to the dance.' 'No – we'll go to the pictures. That's what you'd really like to do, isn't it?' 'No – I'd really like to go to the dance.' It was insufferable. Sometimes we would have to throw something at them to bring them back to the world of real human beings.

Beth and the two Kathleens would make all their

decisions by tossing pennies. But, what to do with Saturdays was very important. Rita and Scottie; Rita and Verona; Verona and Scottie; Rita and I, Lois and Kathleen Lavery – we mixed up and spent our evenings and weekends in changing company.

Lois and Kathleen had something in common: they were both art students. Kathleen had had two years at the Slade and, not particularly wanting to do anything else and being the younger of two sisters, had persuaded her parents to let her stay on for another year. Then she joined the Army. They were a Civil Service family: her father was in the Patent Office, and Joan, her elder sister, was about to be called up. Conscription had begun for young women. Kathleen said she hoped her sister would come and join us here, but we thought that Joan sounded very staid and stodgy, compared with giggly Kathleen. Lois, who was our lance-corporal, was also an artist. She had had an exhibition: living in Oxford must have been a great advantage to her. She lived alone with her mother in one of the dark old houses near Christ Church.

We all told one another tales of home. How we laughed at Lois's description of herself painting a self-portrait: a full-length nude. For modesty's sake and to prevent any opposition from her mother, she had painted at night-time, creeping up to her attic studio when Mother was asleep. It took weeks to finish. The Great Unveiling took place one bright morning, when she broke the news and invited her mother to see it. Imagine her mother's shock – and Lois's. They stared at the painting: it was a magnificent likeness, Lois was a handsome subject, but, having been painted at night, it was yellow!

As we polished our buttons and spat on our shoes, working in the Wren's polish and rubbing and brushing till they gleamed, barracked our beds and swept and dusted our small share of space, we laughed at one another's stories, we grumbled and complained and giggled – and thrived.

It rained eventually, of course, and mizzled and drizzled and kept us off the headland and off the gun-park, and as more and more indoor work was required of us, the IGs began giving their special work to the same small group of us. The building work was finished, and the rest of the detachment came and occupied the other hut in the garden. But those of us who had been there since the start found ourselves with most of the interesting work.

One day George Harding came into the library, sat himself down between Winn and me and boomed: 'How would you like to draw my lobes?' The new arrivals weren't used to him yet, and a few smirks and giggles went round the room, but we managed to keep straight faces and said we would with pleasure.

Kine-theodolite computation is a very straightforward affair, for which every step of the calculation is printed on a set form, but what we got from George was a scribbled formula, in a language that might have been Chinese. What should I do? Let him go, and flounder, and fail, and never be given interesting work again? Or confess and demand an explanation?

'You *are* a Low Show!' he pronounced, and explained. 'You know your dee-wy-be-dee-ex, of course,' pointing to 'dy' over 'dx' among his scribble.

'Oh, yes' I confidently replied, recognizing something vaguely and hoping that there was a book on the calculus somewhere about.

'Do you remember your quadrants?'

'Oh, yes' – because, like Tigger, I felt that here was something I really knew.

He left us with the sketch of how he wanted the function worked out, and the scale he wanted for the graph. We managed the figuring – quite easily as it worked out, but when it came to the drawing, one curve looped round one corner, one skidded across the middle, and a similar unjoined pair scooted around the lower half.

'How did you get that?' We told him.

'I see,' he drawled. 'I see,' his nose getting nearer to the paper. ' "I see," said the blind man, but he never soratall!'

Oh why, in maths, do we have to start going west, anti-clockwise, where my scant knowledge of gunnery had taught me to go clockwise from north? That corrected lobe was the first of many we did for him.

He came in one day when we were dutifully using our

log books to make some long-winded calculations.

'Logs!' he exclaimed scornfully. 'Logs! Never use logs. With logs, inaccuracies are liable to creep in. Use a slide rule!' So, thereafter, for him, we did – and it took a lot of pain out of the work.

'How's the function getting on?' the inimitable voice would demand, and inevitably, one day, 'Where's Miss Brewer, the Function Queen?' He was a great hit with everyone.

We now had our own cook and were eating up at the bungalow. But we pioneers rather regretted the beach hut and our now truly friendly male company. The men's cook was a true soldier in the way my father would approve: 'Take every possible advantage of all available resources.' He certainly did that. It was a time of austerity and shortages: civilians were being told that salt was bad for you, to cloak the absence from it in the shops; nobody had seen an orange or a lemon for two years, and onions seemed to be a thing of the past. So what did he do? He, too, had discovered the wild garlic. We had garlicky mince and garlicky stew, garlicky goulash and garlicky hotpot; and on one shimmering May morning, when the sky was pearl and the sea like silk, we had garlicky porridge for breakfast, when the cooking tins got mixed up.

It was brave of us to attend the Saturday Tenby dances at all, but attend we did, as a change from the cinema and in default of any other amusement. What were we looking for? The sheer pleasure of dancing? Romance, of course. To meet a handsome heart-throb, who could also dance. Life is full of disappointments. Naturally, our dazzling beauty was hidden under those awful stockings and shape-concealing tunics. But we soldiered on.

'In the mood' – quickstep. 'I don't want to set the world on fi-yer!' – foxtrot. 'When they sound the last All-Clear' – waltz. And, terrifyingly, 'Jea-lousy, one two; 'twas only my jea-lousy, one two' – tango. 'Good night, good night, I'll see you in my dreams tonight' – and so on. The dancing, and the inevitable battle of wits.

There are a hundred ways of saying 'No', ranging from

the delicate, to a shy boy, to the emphatic to any persistent swain. It was hardly ever necessary to be downright rude, nor was it called for. This was the world of the dance hall, which was new to most of us. Acquaintance had to be made swiftly, and the chatting-up game was played according to the set rules of the times. A man was expected to 'try it on'. It was supposed to be a compliment to a girl, as well as proclaiming his masculinity, and it was for the girl to say 'No!' No offence was taken, on either side. There it would usually end, and the man would either go and look for someone more accommodating or ask for the next dance; a pleasant evening could be spent, and at the end of it, 'Good night,' and perhaps, 'See you next week?' With no deception on either side. The man knew where he stood, and if he wanted to make a date, you had the confidence to accept. But the ritual was essential.

When the Yanks came later, with disastrous results to British maidens, it was not only their chocolates and silk stockings which seduced the girls. The fact is, they played according to another set of rules. They did not consider it unfair to make hints of love and marriage on first acquaintance, and the whole position became confused.

All this, of course, is about the Girls Who Wouldn't. The Girls Who Would were unmistakeable and did not wait to be asked.

So we played our social game, and the man who danced the 'Last Waltz' with you took you home; or, in our case, to the tailboard of our transport. The sound of hobnails scraping on an unsympathetic floor, to the strains of 'Who's taking you home tonight?' by a weary band, eager to get on to the National Anthem and home, was not exactly the fulfilment of one's dreams, but the journey back to camp was full of compensating laughter, and we swapped many a hilarious experience. Our repertoire of polite rebuffs increased, and the all-time favourite was one of Honor's: 'No, thanks – I'll get plenty of fresh air, in the truck, going home!'

There were genuine romances, of course, and some did find their true loves. Not on that dance floor, but we had many opportunities to meet interesting men, mainly the ones we worked with. Marjorie Simmons married 'Wompo' Key, one of our favourite AIGs; Peggy Carter, sweet Peggy, became Peggy Welch, and she and Ron kept the pub at Penally for many years. Chrissie, smiling Chrissy, also married, and came back after her seventy-two-hour leave more dimpling than ever.

Marjorie,to show us that her romance had not made her soppy, dressed herself up in the exquisite white silk nightgown she had made, clutched its folds round her middle and leapt from bed to bed, all the way round the hut.

Lois discovered the gully. That is, she discovered that it was possible to scramble down to its little beach. It lay on the other side of the headland from the big bay, and all that could be seen from the cliff edge above it was the rock-strewn water's edge. The whole gully itself was like something out of Sindbad: the huge grey boulders filled it as though some giant had hurled them there. But Lois had discovered a route.

And the reward for the squeezing and the climbing, the jumping and the slithering? A smooth, sandy beach, clean and untouched, which, depending on the tide, gave access past or over the smooth shore-line rocks, past creamy spume to a clear blue swimming paradise. Better still, at low tide it was possible to wade past a protruding cliff to another, smaller beach which extended back underneath the cliff path into a cave, where the Enchanted Pool invited us to bathe. It was safest to wade round, rather than try to swim, for strong currents swirled out from it and sucked back down against the rock face. It was much too dodgy for swimmers of my standard.

But – complete seclusion! Lydstep beach was handy, and we were allowed to swim from there, but we didn't all like the shingle beach, and there were always the Eyes. It is nice to be attractive, but no one wants to be as attractive as that. Men were everywhere. They treated us politely individually, but, in a group ... So we were grateful for our little private haven.

7 'Time for some New Thinking'

Lydstep, Summer 1942

At last, we were told what it was that we had come here
for.

There had been threats, we knew, from Hitler that there
was a secret weapon in the making, that would devastate
whole areas and slaughter millions. It was more terrible
than anything anyone had ever seen. The great dread of
the early days of the war, poison gas, had passed away
from us. Now, in May 1942, it was still compulsory to carry
gas masks, but nobody took the things seriously any more.
This new danger that threatened would not, people felt,
be gas; but what could it be?

London had had no air raids at all this past winter.
Other cities had, naval ports and railway centres, but my
corner of the world, where all my family lived, had been
spared. Nevertheless, one could never be sure. It could
always start again tonight. You had to be prepared. But for
what? Unknown to us simple soldier kine ATS, our Secret
Service had had reports of what it might be. The scraps of
information, however, had not made much sense. All the
clues were conflicting.

In fact, as it turned out later, there were three terror
weapons being developed for an onslaught against
London. Only two of them were destined to be finished in
time to use against us, but at that time, in May 1942, we
had no picture of what form this terror might take.
However, the chances were that it would be some sort of
high-explosive missile, directed from a certain place
towards a given target. And as such, it could be engaged
by AA artillery. It was worth a try, anyway. And in the

meantime, if our gunnery could be improved, it would be more effective against the existing type of attack.

Major Mac was a very good expounder of a problem and of ways to combat it. Unfortunately, he had not very much patience, and he told us only once. If you missed it, you missed it. The gist of what he wanted to do was this:

As we knew, there were two main effective types of mobile AA gun: the heavy 3.7-inch and the light 40mm Bofors. There were enough teams now competent to use whatever weapons and ammunition were available, and by the time the overworked factories had produced more, there would be more recruits trained.

'And what does a heavy regiment consist of?' he asked us. (He was a wartime soldier: by profession he was an architect, and his sympathies were not with the traditions of the regular Army.) 'Twelve guns, twelve gunners to each gun, and God knows how many cooks, orderlies, storekeepers, the orderly room, Uncle Tom Cobbley and all. And in some regiments, not one of these has ever touched a gun. Gunners can't use a heightfinder; loaders can't predict a fuze; wartime hasty training can't teach everybody to do everything. They've still got the peace-time attitude of training the gifted to perfection, and. – (I do beg your pardon, ladies).' His smile transformed the sharp face. 'But we've got to change. We're preparing for attack now. The establishment over at Manorbier is now no longer "School of Anti-Aircraft Defence" but "School of Anti-Aircraft Artillery". We've got to change the philosophy. Something like their old tradition: while one drummer boy remains alive, the gun keeps firing.'

He thought he had gone too far and became very matter-of-fact: 'So, it's time for some new thinking. The skills have to be suited to the talent we have, not the other way about. We have been given part of an LAA battery to play with. Six methods of fire-control have been decided upon, and this time it's not to be the general staff who will dictate the method to be adopted, nor the crack troops, but the ordinary gunner, with no natural aptitude for it.

'This is our experiment. And this is to be your job. You are to record their performance and analyse the results. As a start, we are using four squads of five men each, who will be our guinea-pigs. Every man will have at least three runs by each method, at each type of target. We shall vary height and speed, and its course. There will be six methods: four using an open sight, and two, revolutionary for the light gun, using instruments borrowed from the Heavies. One predictor will be modified with something special among its innards. If you think you know what it might be, please don't mention it to the rest of the camp. It is rather sensitive material at the moment. We shall call the trial G.60. You will find the work interesting, I hope.'

He glanced at his watch.

'Nearly coffee time. But I'd better give you some idea of one of the recording drills. Each round in a run will be either too high, too low, too far in front or trailing behind. The form will look like this', and he quickly wrote a list of symbols: H, L, +, −. 'Hits I leave to your own ingenuity.'

Laughter. We all knew how many hits to expect.

'I have been told that you can work well only if you understand what you are doing: Mrs Lang's young women are becoming well known, so I have laid on some gunnery lectures for you. You will find Sergeant-Major Doe a good instructor.'

How refreshing. At last, at last, a man who did not call us 'popsies' or 'your little Ats' or even 'the girls' in his asides to our officers. Here was a man we could respect.

So began our understanding of what we had already seen in practice on the gunpark. Here is the gist of what we learnt.

A Little Bit of Gunnery

(To be skipped by the faint-hearted, but it makes sense of what our work was all about.)

We knew that there were two main kinds of AA batteries: heavy and light. The 4.5-inch was the smallest of the static guns, and we hardly had anything to do with them, the most useful heavy gun being the mobile 3.7 inch. It could engage at a range of 19,000 yards, and it could be fired from its own feet, without the need for emplacements. It fired a heavy shell, as heavy as a man could carry in his arms, and for two good reasons it did not have a percussion fuze. The second reason was that a timed fuze ensured, in theory, the maximum damage to a target, even though it might not actually touch it; it had only to explode fairly near.

The 40 mm Bofors gun was the commonly used light weapon. Its shells were smaller, and if some butterfingers dropped one, it would only blow him up, and not the gun and the rest of the team.

Eyeshooting and a percussion fuze: the Bofors is a gun for the able, the individualist, the champion. Heavy AA gunnery, on the other hand, depends on team work. It is a very involved business. After we had spent a few weeks observing and recording the efforts, we began to wonder why they ever undertook it at all. And I began to understand why the bombers had been getting through so easily.

Imagine. You are trying to hit a moving target. Now, as every schoolboy knows, when you throw a brick at a cat, you have to put on some aim-off. It is no good aiming at where the cat is now: you have to estimate its future position. Your missile takes time to reach its goal, and it does not travel in a straight line. The trajectory is a curve. The shape of the curve depends on how high you throw it, and how fast. Given enough speed, the higher the angle, the further it will go, until you reach about 60 degrees, when it will fall shorter and shorter, until, if you throw it too high, it will come down and land on your head.

But you are not throwing a brick. A gun can be made to change its upward angle, but the missile speed is not changeable at will. The round leaves the gun at maximum speed, or something like it, and slows down according to various laws and atmospheric conditions. The fuze takes time to estimate and set, and the gun takes time to load. This all has to be taken into account. The range – that is, its distance from you – is changing all the time, so the settings that time the fuzes must change all the time.

As a target, a typical target, approaches – not necessarily over your head, its range decreases till it reaches the crossing point, when it begins to recede. So the typical fuze settings for a typical run will decrease, then increase. The settings are measured in seconds. The only factor on the target's flight that can possibly stay the same is its height. Real enemy aircraft don't necessarily travel at a constant height, constant course, constant speed, but you have to start somewhere, for practice purposes.

A gun in action does not stand in a field, all by itself. It needs a source of electric power, so a generator is part of its equipment, feeding the two important directing instruments which are set up within shouting-distance of the gun. A full battery has a height-finder and a predictor for each of its four guns.

Once the height is known, the process can start. The height-finder is a horizontal cylinder, six feet long and five or six inches across. It is supported on a stand, at a suitable height for the use of its telescope sights, one at each end. Its length is the base of a triangle, with the ever-moving target the apex. Halfway along its length there is a spyhole and a small handwheel. Two images may be seen: one from each end of the instrument.

A natural gift, or talent, is called for here. Some people can only see two aircraft jigging about meaninglessly, but there are some, with equally balanced stereoscopic vision, who can see the two images in two different planes. By lining the two to make one and by the wonders of mathematics and mysterious technical marvels, it is possible to read off from a scale a figure which represents the target's height in feet.

This height is fed, by means of the electric cables which snake their muddy way everywhere, into the predictor. This tall metal square box does two important things: it transforms the present position into a future one in relation to the varying distances of the target; and it gives the time in seconds that the round will take to arrive at that future position. It takes five operators to work this, and the most important is the fuze-setter.

The gun-layers have been keeping the gun ahead of the target, by making a pointer follow another pointer round a dial. The constantly altering future position is being fed in from the predictor, where the fuze-setter is watching the fuze drum. This is a cylinder set into the body of the instrument with a graph wrapped round it. A pointer travels along the height line and crosses the time-in-seconds lines. Decreasing time for an approacher; a pause;

then increasing as the target recedes. He has to assess the time it will take to set the fuze on the shell, and to load and fire the gun. He knows his own gun team. He predicts a fuze and gives the shout. When his opposite number at the gun answers: 'Fuze – one three [or whatever] – set!', he gives the order: 'Fire!' It takes the team a few seconds to load, close the breech and get the round off.

Ideally, the gun fires just as the finger on the fuze drum passes the time he has predicted. It is all skill, and rhythm, and working as a team. Some batteries never get it right, but some work as sweet as cream. And sometimes they actually hit the target. Rugby players think they know all about teamwork, but there is nothing to touch an HAA battery at its best.

There are other complications. For instance, every batch of ammunition has a 'fuze factor'. Gunpowder is like the dyes in knitting-wool: no two lots behave exactly the same. An addition or deduction in proportion has to be made for every batch. Also, every gun barrel behaves differently. They twist and droop with age. The wind speed and bearing also affect the round in its flight. So, in order to preserve our sanity, we will not dwell on the Royal Navy's gunnery problems: they do all this on a rolling and pitching deck.

And amid all this noise (the firing, the shouting, the put-put-put of the generators and, in the lulls between runs, the smack-smack-smack of the firing flag's cord as it tried to get away from the flagpole in the stiff wind) we learned to make some sense out of it all and came to understand what part we were playing.

The trial began in fine style. The Bofors is a nippy, handy gun. It can fire single shot, like its heavy brothers, or automatically at two rounds per second, by keeping the firing pedal down. Its shells come in sticks of four; and, not for the benefit of recorders, though we should find it very useful, they have tracers in them. The little tell-tale lights were essential for 'eye-shooting', and they would help us too.

Three types of sight had been prepared. The first was the ordinary forward-area sight (FAS); then there was the Stiffkey Stick, and the third was the cartwheel used in

Naval eye-shooting. Four of Major Mac's six methods were to use these three, using the gun in its traditional role.

The forward area sight was an oval-shaped open sight with two vertical wires dividing the area into three. This drill, we discovered, had a language all its own. 'Three o'clock, 1½!' Twelve o'clock, two!'

Method no.2 used the Stiffkey Stick. This device was based on the idea that if you advanced the gun and banged away at the same spot in space well ahead of the target, it would run into your concentrated area of fire. Then, if it did not, you swung the gun into a new position and fired another static barrage. The Stiffkey Stick was a horizontal bar with a spring handgrip. You gave it one, two or three clicks forward, according to the speed of the target, and the gun moved automatically.

The sight for the third method was the naval cartwheel. Two were used, one for lateral and one for vertical laying.

The fourth method was known as the Joystick. One cartwheel (as in no.3) for the vertical layer, but the lateral gears were disengaged, so that the gun swung freely, and the firer stood on the platform with a rope round his ankle, hauling the gun round himself, putting in the aim-off according to his own instinct and stamping on the firing pedal as well.

The sixth was not ready yet, but the fifth was going to use all the array of heavy gunnery: heightfinder, predictor and all the complications. No.5 was set up, ready for all to see, but no.6 was still a dark secret.

'Remember,' Major Mac had said, 'it's the method, not the man, we're testing.'

Now began the weeks and weeks of labour: recording, observing, filming, evaluating, computing, drawing, analysing. Sending our results to the war office. And all the time, drawing George's Lobes, in preparation for method no. 6.

Soon after we really got started, there was terrible news from North Africa. Tobruk had fallen, and Allied prisoners had been taken. Thirty-three thousand. It was going to be a tougher war than we had thought.

In July the male permanent staff was augmented by heightfinder and predictor teams, a couple of AIGs and some more 'tiffies' – artificers, who really understood the instruments we were all using. And the GL-operators. Radiolocation. Yet another Nissen hut was added to the cluster halfway along the bay, near the NAAFI Nissen.

We spent our midday break there. The penny cup of NAAFI tea was drab in colour but hot and strong, and coffee at three-ha'pence was thick and dark, with plenty of sediment. We missed the YMCA that we had preferred at Manorbier, where coffee, though costing 2 pence, was made with hot milk, and the grounds strained out. Never mind, the company was jolly, and we learned to do swaps with our canteen rations. Those of us who did not smoke – and there were a few – could always find someone who would give us his chocolate coupons.

These were the days of the rhyming craze: 'Come near the heater, Rita!' – 'You look like death, Beth,' – 'I'm a goner, Honor!' I was luckier: 'Have a toffee, Doffy!' (Or even a coffee!)

Half an hour was a pleasant length of time for a morning's break. Plenty of time, after queuing, to drink the coffee and eat the fruit slice or other puddingy cake and to continue yesterday's flirtation or argument.

We girls were now self-sufficient, in our Nissen huts and the bungalow, where we ate now and had our recreation room. Our cook was a Danish girl called Xenia, who, with the orderly, Bing, gave us meals that really tasted of food. Bing's shingled auburn hair and her fine tenor voice had earned her her name. She had a wonderful disposition and had struggled manfully for those early weeks when her work must have been very hard. While the plumbing work went on, she had nothing to use but the rainwater all day. One day, when a dead mouse was found in the butt, she solemnly promised that she would not use that water to make our tea. Only the cocoa.

Only once I remember her being exasperated with us. We had come up for tea, and there was the fire, only just lit, and the two buckets of lukewarm water on the plate, with dry tea-leaves floating about on top.

'Oh, Bing!' I said.

'You get out of my kitchen!' she yelled. 'That'll be all right when it boils!'

We were now entitled to a sergeant again, and Sheila Caws came to join us. She was a big girl, gently spoken, and a fit partner for Marnette Linton, our junior commander, whom we were beginning to respect and admire more every day. Anything with stripes and certainly all officers are a soldier's natural enemy – but Marnette, Sheila, Frosty, Lois? The rules did not seem quite to apply in our leafy haven. Marnette seemed to have the trick of encouraging us, standing between us and the unnecessary petty restrictions that make up Army life. In her quiet Scots voice she fought our battles with the Western Command ATS commander and her underlings, smoothing our relationships with stores and discipline, parades and appearance, and altogether let us enjoy the sensation of being a law unto ourselves in our hideaway. How things were to change, later on!

Frosty left us, and Jessie Wareham arrived. We were beginning to be experienced barrack-room survivors, and a new NCO was to be regarded with suspicion. How could we get this one to do as we wished? How should we mould this one to our ways?

Jessie was different. Older, for one thing. Serious. Small, nut-brown, determined. Bright black eyes, straight black hair. Inscrutable. She handed out written orders, so that you couldn't argue. She would tell a small anecdote and disappear, so that you couldn't respond. We couldn't see her vulnerability: all we could see was a rather stern little face, and a taste for having orders obeyed to the letter. Poor Jessie! We came to like her later on, but she took some getting used to.

All that summer, kine course after kine course came in to Manorbier Camp, each creating another detachment to serve yet another new practice camp, as they sprang up all along the western coast and started to come down the eastern side (Whitby and Weybourne); and there were experimental establishments at Woodyates and Wimborne, all waiting for a kine team.

A new kine instructor stepped in. Evelyn Cochrane had coped heroically with the job for a year, when the greatest pressure was on and a nature brisker than hers would have found it easier. Every few weeks a new set of faces, and after three weeks off they would go and another set come, to be taught the hasty physics, the rule-of-thumb trig and a swift skid over electricity.

Joan Cotter settled very happily into a job that seemed to have been made for her. She was efficiency itself. We saw her often, when we were out at stations and she brought out a group from the course to see the old hands, to show them how it should all be done. There we would be, waiting for the next 'Target – plane – observe!', eating our toast or drinking our tea, ready to jump when the message was received, but this was obviously Not Good Enough for the uninitiated to see, so a code was invented.

When an officer was heading in your direction, there would be a message from CC post: ' "A" station – how many empty containers have you?' This was our signal to put out cigarettes, do up jackets and don caps. It worked very well, it deceived no one, and it saved a lot of embarrassment.

Joan Cotter was bringing more and more kines into the fold. During the course of this year, nearly 200 more were to be added. There were some failures, naturally, and some kines left, but we now had a solid body of 200 or more, increasing all the time, working in different kinds of establishments, in different capacities.

There were some cross-postings from one detachment to another, and we began to feel that we had a little world of our own, and all knew one another.

It was no use our kidding ourselves that we belonged primarily to the Army, doing the Army's work. The plain fact was that we were in the ATS and had to be treated as such, especially by ATS admin. officers.

Our resistance to the general duties officers had not lessened: in fact, it had hardened into a sort of antagonism. It seemed to us that they used their little bit of temporary power as a weapon. After all, we were all only wartime soldiers, and this was not our career for life. The poor little orderlies stood no chance against them at all but were bullied in what we thought was a most unfair way. Luckily for us, we were not harried too much, as they were all in Top Camp and mostly we could ignore them.

But when there was a confrontation, we were not the sort to be put down, for no reason.

It was summer-time, and of our two main preoccupations – getting warm enough and trying to keep clean – our present obsession was the difficulty of getting a bath. The new ablutions block at the bungalow was all right for a wash-down in the morning and a quick lick at night, but that was all. However, while the good weather – the warm weather – lasted, we were quite happy to take a rolled-up towel over the cliffs to Top Camp, where the occupants of the Mae West huts still tolerated us cheerfully: 'Here come the soaks again!'

Marnette was interceding for us down at Lydstep House. Perhaps we might have the use of one of the bathrooms there, she suggested; but of course that was quite against all military precedence and discipline. Besides, there were too many of us. We were privates and other low ranks, and it simply wouldn't do.

In the meantime, the ATS admin. section up at the camp discovered that, against King's Regulations, which lay down that all military personnel must be paraded to the bath-house twice a week, kine personnel seemed not to have had a wash for six months. Something must be done.

Down near the beach at Lydstep, under the lee of the headland, were some old stables. It was a tall, square building, and we knew that the men of the permanent staff had run a water pipe into it, improvised some sort of wood-fired heating and put in a light. We asked them, jocularly, if they could contrive something of the sort for us. They were very helpful and offered to let us share it with them. Ho, ho. Very amusing.

In September a notice appeared on the Daily Orders, Part One, issued from ATS Western Command, Manorbier, something to this effect: 'The 6th KT (Lydstep) will parade outside quarters at 6.30 p.m. for bath parade. Corporal – will see that all personnel parade with soap and towel, and wear PT shoes. Facilities have been made available to ATS on Tuesday and Thursday evenings.'

We fell about, delighting one another with many sarcastic remarks, then applied ourselves to the usual problem: how to get out of it. If someone was going to suffer, it wouldn't be us.

'What showers, anyway? I see no showers.'

'They can't mean – no! They couldn't possibly ...'

But Lois said that all our hut had better be the first squad and that if we directly disobeyed an order, it could make things very difficult.

The weather was fine, for once, and when the GD corporal arrived, we had already fallen in. We were going to be so virtuous and smart, she would wonder what we were up to.

'Move to the right in threes. Right – turn!'

We managed to keep straight faces and stamped our plimsolls on the ground in unison, like good little auxiliaries, clutching our towels under our arms. It was, as we had feared, to the Gunners' Splash that we were headed, and the corporal herself opened the door. What met her in there made even her recoil a bit. And now our good humour evaporated. Our exaggerated 'obey to the letter' technique that we had planned was designed to drive a nervous NCO mad, but this was no longer a joke.

She marched us in and closed the door. In the grey gloom, faintly lit by a single sad-looking bulb, we could just make out a row of metal clothes-pegs, across the middle of the space, then the greasy wooden bench under them, and steel cages under that. But the smell hit us, all at once. It was not a latrine smell; it was not rotting vegetation or rats, alive or dead, but a sickly smell of corruption, like something from the bottom of the sea.

Two or three lungfuls of this, I thought to myself, and we'll have to invent a new drill: vomiting by the left, in threes.

But there was no time to think. The corporal was brisk: 'First six strip off. Put your things on that bench and get into the showers. I'll give you three minutes.'

Showers! Six open stalls gaped before us, darker and danker than the rest of the place. Habit moved us to obey, but something stronger held us fast. Strip. In that clammy hole? And actually to put your naked foot on that slimy floor ...?

'Get on with it. Put your towels down there.'

We were not civilians, who even in time of war might

possess a bath towel, a hand towel and one for the face and one for the hair and one for the beach, and another clean set in the airing-cupboard. We were ATS privates, whose other towel was away at the laundry, and this was all we had for all uses until Friday. None of us moved.

We began to mutter: 'I'm not going in there' – 'I'm not taking my clothes off in here' – 'You can't call that a shower' – 'It's disgusting.'

'These are the men's showers. They have been kind enough to let you have them twice a week.'

An officer, whether commissioned or not, who starts arguing with subordinates when they are insubordinate is lost, and we knew it. If only we could think of just the right line to take.

'Oh, you – you kines! You're all the same. I'll put you on a charge. I'll put you all on a charge.'

'We'll appeal to higher authority. You can see for yourself.' This was Beth, who now had her stripe. She was the one who said, 'We're entitled to see our own officer.'

It stopped the girl in her tracks, and she considered this.

How it happened, I forget, but Marnette came to sort out our troubles. She took one look at the dingy scene, caught a whiff of the abominable smell, trod delicately on the unspeakable floor and challenged us.

'I have been told that you have a complaint,' she said, quite quietly. She once more inspected the scene in all its details, giving no hint of what she might be feeling. 'What do you complain of?'

'Ma'am,' said Beth, who years later was to be a magistrate, 'there are no curtains.'

No curtains! Oh, good old Beth!

Junior Commander Linton's eyes did not give her away, but her mouth trembled. We had lived up to her expectations of us. She dismissed the parade, and Western Command allowed us to go one more day unwashed. The corporal was spoken to kindly and sent back to camp.

There was a lot of activity around the shower block for a day or two after that, and a week later we paraded again. By this time the weather had been wild once or twice, and we were beginning to think that a shower without half-an-hour's cliff scramble for it might be acceptable.

The lamp was no brighter, but the place had been transformed. The walls had been scraped of the excrescences which had harboured who-knows-what, and whitewashed; the stalls had been scrubbed clean, the nasty peg arrangement had been replaced by a solid stack of wooden lockers (which, incidentally, made a screen before the doorway), there were duckboards on the floor and, lo and behold, pretty flowered curtains hung at each shower stall – the sort that are used in Army medical centres. And there was a different smell. Of clean water.

We capitulated and obeyed. But we chalked it up to ourselves, this time.

Beth's stripe was for being our new physical training instructor. A PT corporal had been coming over from Top Camp to give us a few physical jerks for ten minutes after breakfast, but now we could have our PT early. And eat afterwards.

'Up, up, up!' She was worse than any bugler. Buglers don't come into the hut and wriggle your toes. 'Come on, you young, strong, healthy girls!' She was enthusiastic and unmercifully energetic in the morning. 'Out onto the lovely green grass! I've chased the cows away!'

And we would struggle into our shorts, hop over the stile and cavort in the dew for a quarter of an hour.

Working-hours grew longer and longer, and the days grew shorter and shorter. Soon evening work was taken for granted, and as the results proliferated, there was more and more paperwork all the time.

Winn and I were spending most of our working day in the library, not going out to stations much and only occasionally working on the gun-park. Sometimes we went up onto the headland, where all sorts of strange machines and instruments were swinging about and doing odd things. I was up there one day, with a drawing-board under my arm, when the wind nearly carried me out to sea. My cap flew off, my hair ribbon escaped, but sympathy was not on the programme. The grass was wet, the cables were half-hidden in it, and Val Cox caught her foot in one and fell over.

'Stop playing the fool, Cox,' commanded our gallant,

handsome young captain i/c GL recorders. 'The run's about to begin.'

We were attending the beginning of great things. Nothing less than the adaptation of radar to gunnery weapon-control. Not just as a warning device, which was wonderful enough, but to use it to direct fire. The RAF had it, and it was becoming noticeable that our aircraft were as successful in the dark as in daylight.

Remember 'Cat's Eyes' Cunningham? He was a combat pilot so singularly successful in night fighting that a myth had to be invented. A small fact was turned, by the Ministry of Information, into a large lie. It is true that carrots contain a substance that is extremely good for eye health; doctors were already advising their patients to eat plenty of carotene, and out of this ... Newsreels showed aircrews eating raw carrots, implying that this could give a certain proportion of the population night vision.

'Try it – you never know – you might be one of the number!'

Many people did. Carrot-consumption went up dramatically. And, in the absence of oranges, it was probably very good. But night vision? Years later, some there were who still believed in it, long after the secrets of radar had been revealed. But at that moment it was a little light-heartedness in a disheartening world. Nowhere was there good news from the battlefronts.

Work went on. Honor and Rita were getting fed up with all the standing-by, waiting between showers and mists for something to happen on the gun-park. Life began to be frustrating.

Winn and I were usually the last ones left in the library at the end of the day's work, for we usually did the final graph. Many people can draw a straight line, freehand, by putting the pencil at the beginning, fixing the eyes on the end and having faith, but I at that time had a happy knack of being able to smooth and draw a curve, if I brooded a minute or two and then concentrated on not thinking. Whoosh! And it nearly always worked.

I was thus brooding one evening, when George Harding came in with two presents for me, one in each hand. 'French curves,' he said. 'Make a hard life easier.' They looked like a pair of demented set-squares whose edges had somehow spread out into fantastic curves, one with a curlicue on one corner like the top of a violin.

The next day he called in again, to see how we were getting on. As it happened, the entire detachment was in. He watched my clumsy fumblings for a minute or two, his nose drawing nearer and nearer to the paper, then pronounced, in a rising crescendo, 'The Man Who Keeps His French Curves Still – Is Doomed!'

How we all loved George!

8 'Don't Be Too Discouraged'

Lydstep, Autumn and Winter 1942

Under Marnettes's benign regime, there was a pleasant custom regarding coming back from leave. Our passes gave us ten days. Leave was a Privilege, not a Right, but usually we were granted it, according to a roster that was published and altered according to some of our requests. Seven days every three months, plus a forty-eight-hour pass that could be sacrificed and added to it. Add the Sunday, and you have ten days. By travelling at night, we could wangle the utmost out of it, but this meant arriving at Tenby or Penally at about seven in the morning of the first day back on duty. After a night probably spent sitting on a kitbag in the corridor, we were not on top form. This is where Marnette's kindness came in. Some trivial extra duty would be saved up for the homecomer, and that counted as a morning's work.

Mine, on one notable occasion, was ready made for me. I was to go down to the stores, a Nissen hut down on the foreshore, and collect some Vim. Vim did not come to the Army in nice little cylinders with holes in their shiny tops. It came loose, like everything else. Unused dustbins were supplied to every new cookhouse, to be filled with flour, rice, sugar, dried egg and so on. If you wanted baking powder, you took your own basin for it. If you wanted scouring powder, you took your own basin for it.

I was always on leave when anything memorable happened. Poor Bing, in her enthusiasm at being left to make a lovely sponge pudding, had put her hand into the wrong basin, so I was sent the next morning to replace the Vim. The stores bombardier was, like many of his rank, sarcastic about girl soldiers,and he was ready to make suitable remarks.

'What the hell do they do with it?' he grumbled. 'They had some only two days ago.'

'They ate it for their dinner,' I truthfully replied.

'Don't you sauce me!' he roared.

I had my revenge by disdaining to explain.

When Marnette told us that she was leaving to go to another unit, where her knowledge of Russian would be put to good use, we were desolated. We did not just like her: we adored her.

Which made things very difficult for Mrs Lang, her successor, who came as a stranger, though some of us had seen her once or twice. We were ready to resist any changes that a new broom might bring; we were ready to resent anything from Marnette's supplanter, and we were ready to hate the very physical presence of anyone new.

When our new commanding officer first set eyes on us, we must have looked a rather slomocky lot. We still had not received our proper boots, and from the chinstrapped caps to the sloppy gumboots we must have caused her enthusiastic heart to sink. She did so want her girls to be the pride of the service.

The idyll was over. Our new CO's voice was everywhere.

'Goldson!' Winn always hated wearing a hat, and it seemed reasonable to her that, for the two minutes that it took us to get down to the house, a cap was not necessary. 'Goldson! Cap!'

One cold windy morning, at early parade: 'Brewer!' Whatever had I done now? 'That scarf!' It was Honor, of course, who had the scarf – not me. But then, everyone mixed us up.

She put notices up. Hand-written ones, everywhere. 'Don't do this. Don't do that.'

She made Lois write another notice for the library door: 'Out of bounds – to virtually everybody.'

Major Mac and George Harding pretended to be afraid of her and made a game of dodging in when she was not there to intercept their direct access to us, so that she distributed the work. She reorganized the library blackout duty, to our entire dissatisfaction. The big panels were about ten feet high in that great room, and whoever was Duty Aux. usually got a friend to help; now that was out.

We fed our grumbles with regrets and ruses, like naughty boys. But Marnette's successor would have stood no chance with us, whoever she was.

However, efficient she was. We were not the only ones she rousted. Very soon after her arrival, electric light came to our Nissen huts, lino for the floors; and a squad of gunners repaired a stone hut in the garden for a wood store for us. (Wooding was our delight and recreation, in working hours. In between times, little groups of us went into the Wild Wood and gathered sticks and twigs and, more boldly, whole logs.)

Some of our freedoms remained to us, but some of the girls felt the restrictions sorely. More and more we sought the warmth that was to be found at the top of the lane. Mrs Walters' café was no more than a small house that in peacetime had been used as a shop. The front room opened straight from the road, and it was now packed with small tables and chairs – as many chairs as could be crammed in. The back room was almost entirely occupied by one large table and, in the middle of what space there was, the stove. Gently bubbling pans of bacon, over the blue flames of the three-burner oil stove, gave a mixture of aromas that persists in the memory, with power still to evoke the love and welcome that radiated from it.

Mrs Walters was a sturdy, brown-eyed, smiling woman with time for every one of us. Men from Top Camp with their girlfriends, men from Top Camp without their girlfriends. Always a few of us, escorted or unescorted. Some of the Trials Wing men, and an occasional civilian lorry-driver.

The stove purred, and the blue flame danced every time the door opened and someone else came in. Fried bread, bacon and whatever else she could get. Sometimes the gunners would bring her mushrooms they had picked; sometimes tomatoes would be on the menu. Eggs were a rarity, reserved for birthday parties in the back room ('for my specials'). She never chased us out when we had finished eating. An evening at 'the shop' was an evening. If more came in, more chairs were found from somewhere, and everyone squeezed up.

Her daughters flitted in and out, serving and clearing, bringing more tea, washing up, chattering and laughing, while their mother presided over all.

But we could not have every evening free, to seek comfort and company.

I was seething. It was ten o'clock at night, and I was still working. The worst of it was, it was my own fault. Nobody could I blame but my own self. Idiot!

The trial was finished, and the tabulated results were due to go for photo-statting in the morning. The sheet before me was half the size of the table, with about twenty columns and about fifty lines of figures to be filled in. The paper was a pale buff colour, smooth and translucent; the writing instrument a mapping pen dipped in Indian ink.

My figures were pleasant to look at. I was proud of my work. But it was late, the fire was getting low, the sheet still only half-filled and my sore finger getting more and more inky. The figures on the copy sheet were beginning to dance. But it had to be done before morning.

There was the sound of cars outside: the officers had been out to dine somewhere. All right for some, I thought, savagely. Voices in the corridor.

'There's a light on in there ...' Laughter, and the door opened. 'What's this?'

'Brewer! Isn't it time for roll call?'

That was the last straw. I did not spring up from my seat for her but just went on writing.

Major Mac came in. In full fig, he looked as only a kilted military man can look, and he strode in, took one look and said, 'We'll send it by the afternoon bag. You can finish it in the morning. It's coming well.'

It had been ready to send that morning. He had come to look at it almost finished, and then: 'It looks a bit squiffy to me.'

The paper we were supplied with came plain, not lined or squared, and all the guidelines had to be measured and drawn in. I had cut the piece off the roll and had spent all the previous day ruling it up, writing the headings and filling in the figures.

And this morning: 'a bit squiffy'?

The whole thing was out of true. Instead of squaring it up with a protractor, I had just measured from the cut edge, which was not quite straight. So the whole thing was on the slant.

For the sake of the record, Winn measured it for me before I screwed it up, and it proved to be a quarter of a degree off. A quarter of one degree. And he could see it, straight away.

There had been another occasion, when his eyes swept a whole sheet of figures that Winn and I had worked on. They were averages, the results from the different firing methods used by the four squads. Out of all that mass, he noticed one oddity and queried it. We checked and found that it was a single observation instead of an average, when the weather had stopped firing for about a week, and it had been forgotten. You come to love working for someone like that, whom you can admire. I was not the only one of his little team who was devoted to him.

We saw less and less of 'Hoppy' – Major Hopkinson, the shy scientist of Trials Wing. He became more and more remote from us, more absent-minded than ever, working day and night on the calculations that might save all our lives.

In October our boots arrived. They were waiting for us at Manorbier. But rather than let us waste a morning 'drawing stores', the stores corporal was ordered down to us with a selection so that we could be fitted. We had already sent a list of sizes required, having been told to order two sizes larger than our shoes, to make room for socks and a bit of movement.

The unfortunate woman came into the library, dragging her box, and held up the first pair.

'Anyone for 5s?' No. The smallest that any of us had asked for was 6. 'Any 6s?' Yes, three of us. She was beginning to look worried. 'They told me to bring some 7s.'

'Yes, here.' Just one.

'And I brought one pair of 8s.'

'Here!' 'Here!' 'Here!' 'Didn't you bring any 9s?'

'9s?' She was almost in tears. 'I'm new to this job. I saw the sizes you'd asked for. They told me it was you lot having us on again. I was told to bring boots to a squad of girls. No one told me you were a lot of elephants!'

It was sorted out after a day or two, and after all we had to go to the stores for the rest of our goodies. There were leather gaiters, fastened with two buckles, rather stiff and cumbersome, but nothing that a year or two's polishing couldn't put right, we made sure to tell each other. Someone in a fit of imaginative generosity had wangled from central stores the wonderful gloves – shearling. These were finger mittens made of first-shorn sheepskin, with the outside inside and the bluish suede outside. They had a cotton bag mitt, lined with the same shearling suede, which covered the fingers or fastened back with a big press stud on the wrist. 'Spankers', we called them. They were a wonderful comfort, and it meant that our days of soggy feet in sodden shoes, and freezing hands in damp woollen gloves, were over. The socks were pale blue, too; men's normal issue grey wool. We tried them on, and once more those of us who were not of official kine stature were in trouble. They were not just a bit too big: it was ridiculous. So a new task lay before us. Unpick half the foot, re-knit a toe and finish with a graft. But they are marvellously comfortable to wear.

Some had knitted socks before, some had not. How do you start the graft? Purl take it off, knit keep it on? Front row or back row? Oh, hell! I've got an odd number of stitches. Trial and error proved it to be: knit take it off from the front row, first. I think.

We learned a lot of domestic skills from one another: things our mothers should have taught us. Honor was the champion fire-lighter. She taught me how to get a blaze in a matter of moments, making a sort of 'house that Jack built' with sticks over crumpled paper, a few sticks across the top, and little bits of coal poked in, carefully preserving a good draught. Some of the others were all right with the fire, having been Girl Guides, but I was the one who taught Val Cox how to scrub a floor without getting herself marooned. Great joke, when this was remembered later, when we all knew one another better. Doffy, teaching someone to do something domestically useful!

We did not mind barrack nights now so much: we had milked all the fun out of fifty different ways of sneaking out, and we regarded it as part of the inevitable routine. So we made the best of a bad job, and stayed in.

The great thing was to get up a fug in the hut. Have plenty of fuel in – wooding expeditions had produced a good store of logs. The men had a band saw down near the beach and taught us how to use it without cutting ourselves in half. The small black stove glowed sometimes. Coal and wood in alternate layers make a very good recipe.

Xenia used to let us get our own supper. She put a great block of cheese on the scrubbed kitchen table, bread, marge, also in a hard block, tins of condensed milk, and cocoa. The real old-fashioned stuff, with its cocoa-butter still in it. Almost impossible to dissolve, but we discovered the secret. Into the pint all-purpose mug, a good spoonful of cocoa, a little drop of cold water and stir like mad. It must be cold water. Then add boiling water by degrees and slosh in half a tin of Nestlé's milk. The water buckets were on the kitchen range, but we usually kept any titbits in the hut, to augment our feast.

Sometimes we had guilty pangs, when we thought of the people at home and how they were managing on so little, how a tin of milk or a bit of dried fruit was so precious. Xenia knew how we felt, but it was more than anyone's life was worth to try to take any of this plenty home with us on leave. Once she gave me 'to eat on the train', instead of the expected sandwiches or cake, a handful of dried apricots. A nice big handful. My mother, who had managed to save a bit of sugar, rejoiced.

Another winter engulfed us, and more mud. Lydstep mud is different from the red mud of Manorbier. It does not stain, but it is stickier. Rita and I found an old pram chassis down near the beach, and we carried pebbles up on it and made a cobbled doorstep for the hut. It was a great improvement.

We were trying to get used to the boots. They were of good quality,of the type that male officers wore. From our best bootmakers. Mine were from White's. They were brown, like our shoes, which in itself indicated a good-quality leather. (My father, when he bought shoes, always bought brown ones, and if he wanted them black, he stained them.) These boots were lined with fine kid and were as comfortable as any boots could be, for people who had never worn them before. The soles were leather, naturally, reinforced with steel horseshoes on the heel and tips on the toes. They came high up the calf, fastened with laces. Eleven pairs of holes!

They were a lovely support to the ankles, and I came to like them for scrambling over the cliff-tops on the way to work, feeling braver and stronger in slacks and boots, averting my terrified eyes from the cliff edge. Kathleen and I were a great help to each other, if we could contrive to go on duty together. I helped her past the cows in the field, and she encouraged me along the slithery bits, over the gully and across the little stream on its precarious stepping-stones.

We had been trained to do any of the kine work, but the pressure grew, and it was more efficient to specialize a bit. Up at Top Camp was the kine darkroom, presided over by one Penny Pool, sergeant-in-charge. She was a gifted photographer and did a little free-lance portrait work. She took a very pleasant one of me, in my dress fore-and-aft cap. The course photos that we all had were her work, too. She was very possessive of her dark-room and never welcomed a succession of us, messing up her chemicals, tangling up her Correx and generally getting in her way. She used the time-and-temperature method of developing, which she preferred to do in absolute darkness, instead of with the 'safe' light, for better results.

'But, how can you read the clock, Penny?' we asked her.

She had an extraordinary talent. Two, in fact. She could count time in seconds, up to ten minutes, with a latitude of no more than a second or two; and, more important, she could think about something else while she did so. We used to make her perform this party-piece for newcomers, during lulls in the firing on the gun-park, and she never failed. By a strange coincidence, she was also very sensitive to temperature. Where some people have the gift of absolute pitch, she had absolute temperature. She was independent of clock and thermometer and worked in the dark quite happily. But she had to have a partner who could work with her. Some people lose their balance in the complete dark, some forget where things are, and she was very impatient. So Ruth Rich, who opted for dark-room duty while others were having their tea, instead of having to work in the evenings,more and more became Penny's regular mate.

We all found boots uncomfortable at first. They needed a lot of breaking in. And they certainly did not add to our womanly charms. A whole social history could be written about footwear in the thirties. Women's fashions, especially in the summer and in the evenings, were no more than pretty little rags, and a good dressmaker could imitate the latest styles, but shoes were the give-away. Taste as well as quality sorted the sheep from the goats.

Daintily shod feet were not simply vanity: they were a social statement. It was a great sacrifice to us to be seen in these clod-hoppers. And it was something that Ruth could not bear. She complained that the boots hurt her feet; well, they hurt all our feet. I developed two corns, one on each little toe, which stayed with me for the duration. Winn suffered and worked very hard at trying to soften her boots, but they always gave her trouble.

Ruth went to the MO and told him the old, old story, and he believed her. I am not saying that she wasn't more sensitive than the rest of us, just that at that time we thought she'd pulled a fast one. It is quite true that she did very little outdoor work, and boots were not so necessary to her; but we thought it unfair that she should go around looking like a human being, while we had to stomp our way through duty hours, regardless. So, when her unspeakable disaster struck, we were not too sympathetic.

The cookhouse down the beach naturally attracted wild things now that it was cold weather, and whispers went round that rats had been seen down there. Ruth was a great wheedler, and she always went to the Lydstep stores, which was kept by a bombardier, rather than the one up at the camp, which was run by women. She was on her way along the little path between some bushes that led to the store hut when we heard piteous screeching.

'What's Ruth up to now?' would have been the first thought of anyone nearby.

But, poor girl, a rat had run up her trouser leg and was biting her frantically, and she was screaming and trying to get hold of it without being sick or fainting. How she was rescued, I don't know. It made us all wary, but wartime breeds callousness. It couldn't have happened to anyone who wore boots and gaiters, we said. She was quartered in the second of the two huts, and those of us in the first one hardly ever saw her after that. She used to take her dog for long walks, and sometimes took a weekend off and stayed in one of the expensive hotels in Tenby. She became more of a mystery than ever.

But it put us on our guard. One evening, a small furry form was seen, crossing the path from the hut to the bungalow. 'Come on!' we shouted and, picking up sticks and whatever we could, chased the thing. Rats! Up near our hut! It dodged us and came into the hut, and its eyes stared at us from the corner, near Beth's bed.

'That's when they're dangerous! Careful!'

'Don't let it go! What shall we do?'

'Hit it!'

Verona thinks that it was her weapon that finished the rat off. We put the blackouts up and the lights on. Verona sat on Kath's bed, crying. We all felt sick. It was a baby rabbit.

We had no more rat-hunts. Back to the 'rat sandwich' days.

The obsession grew with the volume of work. G.60 tried to become G.60/1, with the radio-controlled predictor added to our five fire-control methods.

'Don't be too discouraged if we don't get it right first time,' Major Mac said to us. 'There is some point at which it must come to, and all we have to do is keep on at it till it does.'

That's all! It started again: the firing, the frustrations, the standing-by, watching mad GL sets that didn't know their left from their right, jiggling about and making the guns twirl about in a crazy parody of battle. There was the aircraft, miles out to sea, and there were the guns, jinking about, facing inland. Radar is wonderful, but it does not think in the round: its world is confined to half the circle, and it doesn't know which half is which. Then the mist, or rain, would come down. The feverish finishing-off of results in the evening; and next morning, all to be done again.

Sometimes there was a clear day: everyone to Top Camp, where guns could actually be fired. Occasionally some good rounds, to cheer everyone up, then: 'Stoppage – held!' And another delay.

The scientific approach was obviously everyone's duty, but you couldn't help favouring one system over another. It was easy to be impartial in the library, surrounded by sheaves of numbers waiting to be sorted out, but out on the Wet Wild Gun-Park, in the Wet Wild Sunshine, in all the noise and confusion, it was not so easy to stay cool. We each cheered (silently, of course) for the gunsight or the gunner that we fancied.

All in all, the Stiffkey Stick appealed to most. It was spectacular, it didn't look intellectual, and most of the men could make an encouraging noise with it. On the other hand, Gunner Peacock, leader of 'W' Squad, using the Joystick, mounted on the platform like a charioteer, lugging the barrel round in great leaps, using the single cartwheel sight, often inspired an irresistible audible cheer. He scored hits. But it was the method, not the man, that we were testing.

Method 6 was tested, and its results were drawn out. Kathleen was our draughtswoman, and Winn, she and I tried to fudge the scale and the plotting, so that it at least looked as though guns and radar were looking at the same target. It was all hopeless. The IGs were sitting up later and later; more adjustments were made to the headland instruments; time was moving on, and everyone was getting tired.

The radar device that was being developed was no longer the simple little blip-on-a-tube that Honor and I had seen that night at Manorbier: it was a much more complex affair.

To detect, and follow. That was the first main difference. Not only to tell but to hook on and track the target automatically: that was now the aim. And, having done that, to feed the continuous information into a sympathetic tube fitted into a predictor, so that future position was fed through all the time. Straight to the guns. But, alas! Machines have not the skills of men. They can be quick and have infinite patience, but they have no flair. And yet, even we could see that the days of Gunner Peacock, the shining warrior, were passing.

It went on and on. On and on. Only one incident stands out in all the boring tedium.

A whole lorry-load of precious cathode-ray tubes was expected to be delivered. They were like gold dust. It was a day late, and no news. We had seen a tube being unpacked; it had its own little crate, with spiral springs from all corners making a kind of cradle for the fragile, awkwardly shaped thing.

A lorry-load, representing our whole supply for the trial, was somewhere halfway up some Welsh mountain. Then word came. There had been an accident. The whole lot had crashed down a precipice, and the driver had been killed.

'Did the tubes survive?' asked the AIG quartermaster.

'Yes, every one.'

'Thank God for that! That's all right, then.'

If the future of radar control had been in the hands of Winn and me, it would never have got past the Lydstep headland. We didn't like it. The plots it gave were like the track of a demented chicken, over-correcting first this way, then that. A man learns to follow a moving line by reducing his mistakes after experience; but a robot is stupid, and if it loses the target, it swings back so vigorously that its correction is worse than the original deviation. And once it starts jigging, there is no stopping it. It was very disappointing. All that work, and all that wonderful inventiveness! We could have cried.

The days darkened, tempers got shorter, the news from the Africa campaign was worse every day.

Then, on 2 November, news came through of the Battle of Alamein. It was unbelievable. But it was true. The tide had turned. The tide had truly turned. It was our first success of the war. Church bells, that had been silent, held back in case of invasion, rang out in celebration.

Alamein Night. Alamein Night in wardrooms, messes and canteens.

It was good news at last. Perhaps it was a good omen for us, here in our fog and confusion. Our activity went from fever to frenzy, and the moment came when the first target run was called.

It was unbelievable. The rounds were all line-of-sight skimmers, every one. Unheard-of. And a fair-and-square, middle-of-the-target HIT. So off went the plane, home. Five minutes to discuss it. Buzz, buzz. Buzz, buzz. Everyone had an opinion. Back came the plane, with a new flag. Another successful run, with a hit on the corner. Another run; another hit. Incredible.

Then it started to rain.

As usual, beginner's luck does not always follow through, but that day was the turning of the corner. After the first euphoria, all that it meant for us was more and more to do. One flash of inspiration by a genius means only one thing for everyone else: work, and more work, and with all the blazing talent that surrounded us, we were in for a busy time.

Christmas at Lydstep was to be the real, traditional Army celebration. The highlight, to which all Other Ranks looked forward with glee, was to be the Christmas dinner, served by the officers.

Christmas Eve was declared a holiday, with various sporting activities arranged at Top Camp. There was to be a fifteen-minute-each-way football tournament, and we all prepared our fanciful colours for the occasion. There was to be transport laid on to Tenby, morning, afternoon and evening. And in the evening, carols in the Lydstep NAAFI, just along the beach. On the day itself, time to get to church if we wanted to (no church parade) before the dinner at one o'clock. Balloons and decorations appeared from nowhere, and we all went 'wooding' for logs and evergreens. We began to feel festive.

A dance was to be held for all permanent staff, all ranks,

on Christmas night, in the library, and on Boxing Day more sports, including a shooting competition. In the evening, a whist drive; and the next day was Sunday. Four days' holiday. What joy, what rapture!

But first, Christmas Eve. After the sporting triumphs, the carol singing. We prepared our sentimental tears, ready to sing lovingly and lustily and sentimentally the wonderful old favourites.

As a small group of us approached the Nissen hut in the trees, we could hear that they had started without us. The way was dark, the weather cold. The scene that smote us as we opened the door nearly drove us out again. But it was warm inside, and there would be coffee and mince pies.

One of the gunners was bashing the piano, and drunken voices were belting out a parody of 'We Three Kings'. Then it was 'Good King Wenceslas', with all the actions – by those still capable. It was not at all the sort of Christmas Eve we had expected. ('Why not?' my father asked me, a fortnight later, when I was on leave. 'Of course, they'd be drunk. It was Christmas Eve, wasn't it?') Coughing in the smoke and gasping in the fumes, we joined in, learning all the actions, crying 'Encore!' with the rest, doing justice to 'God rest ye merry' and finishing with 'The Miner's Dream of Home' and 'Nellie Dean'. What can you do? And we had to admit, it was funny.

The real carols, at the little church at Manorbier the next morning, had an added zing we had not noticed before.

Dinner was a great occasion. We, the lowly, were invited to sit down at the transformed tables; and all our tormentors and all our slave-drivers, as well as all our favourites, came and waited upon us. It was most enjoyable. Major Mac made sure to call Winn and me 'Miss Goldson' and 'Miss Brewer' with such a twinkle,and Major Harding boomed from the other end of the table, 'Do I detect my Function Queen under that delectable hat?' It quite made my day. Even Mrs Lang joined in all the fun and laughter. We decided that she must be human, after all.

The dancing was fun, too.

'You are my sunshine, My only sunshine; You make me

happy, When skies are grey,' we sang, and 'A B C D E F G H I got a gal – in Kalamazoo,' and 'Give me land, lots of land, and the starry skies above; Don't fence me in …'

The musicians were up in the gallery. The fire crackled and the holly singed. It really felt like Christmas Day.

The next morning, we girls submitted ourselves to the helpful hands that taught us how to fire a .22 rifle. We were a shy generation, men as well as girls, and it all caused much merriment.

9   'I've Got a Secret!'

Lydstep, Winter to Summer 1943

One option for a cold night was to go to Manorbier Camp, to the Garrison Theatre. Emlyn Williams brought us *Night Must Fall*; there were ENSA shows. It was really quite unfair to call it 'Every Night Something Atrocious'. Sometimes the camp got up its own show; and Sybil Thorndike gave us *Medea*.

There might be a concert in the YM, or a threepenny dance in the NAAFI. Old Stephen was not a very romantic partner: he spent all his thoughts on his ageing parents, he had a face like the moon, there were the beginnings of a paunch on his thick body, but he danced like an angel. He told me tales of the old-fashioned waltz competitions, where you practised with egg-shells under your heels, and the dip and sway of the dance was all arms and shoulders, the heels never touching the floor. He would never presume to ask a girl out for the evening but would come and beg a dance, here and there. He always gave me the old-style waltz, and we spun and twirled in woolly khaki and lace-up shoes on a floor sticky with spilt beer to dreamy Strauss tunes, played by really a quite reasonable band.

One advantage of spending the evening over at the camp was that it meant going warm to bed. The shop at Lydstep gave us a cosy evening, but it was a chilly scramble down the lane in the gusty dark, and getting into bed still shivering. But the half-hour walk from Manorbier, though starting just as cold, went through stages of discomfort. First the shock and the shivers. Then getting into the swing: a simple stoical switch-off of feeling took you along for five minutes or so. Another five, and it was almost bearable, and for the rest of the time natural warmth began to take over and beat the cold and the wind. It took the last five minutes to bring the blood into fingers and toes.

Bing would have a bucket of hot water on, for cocoa, but we hardly ever needed a hot water bottle on these nights. A crowd of us would come home singing along the dark lanes, then go to bed, thinking of the people at home. My mother was recovering from her operation, and I prayed that there would be no more air raids that winter.

It was too much to hope for. The RAF had at last managed to make bombing raids on Berlin. The Luftwaffe could attack our cities easily, from their bases on the French coasts, so near our shores – but from our aerodromes, Berlin was an impossibly long way away. Then, at last, long-range bombers made a devastating attack on the German capital, in the early days of 1943. There were two retaliatory raids on London in January, but with very little effect, now that our pilots were equipped with radar, and the AA were more organized.

We girls, who had joined up to fight the foe – or come as near fighting as we could, thought of our families,. husbands, boyfriends, in danger and far away, while we were here in a place of complete safety and seeing none of the horrors. But all the time, through all our pleasures and grumbles and time-wasting chores, there was one thought, waking and sleeping: to get the war over, by our work and by taking part in the National Effort, as it was now called. By going without luxuries, by not using petrol and not using too much coal ('Is your journey really necessary?'), going without sweets and living on dull, filling food. By bathing in five inches of water; by writing on both sides of the thin, rough, off-white wartime paper; by managing on one tablet of soap once a fortnight; by Keeping Mum; by keeping cheerful. Defeatism was a social sin. Most of our generation still use only half-an-inch of toothpaste on the brush.

By saving for Victory; by buying National Savings stamps; by Digging for Victory. Every civilian now, as well as doing his (or her) full-time essential War Work as well as being a fire-watcher, warden, First Aid rescuer or special constable, was expected a dig up his lawn and grow vegetables. The whole population, with the exception of the first of the spivs, was engaged in Total War.

'What would you be doing, if it wasn't for the war?'

We were all hastily changing into battledress, standing round the stove, because the sun had come out after all, and Saturday afternoon was cancelled.

'Oh, I'd be ...'

And we all stared at one another, trying to imagine what peacetime was like, when there was no all-consuming passion to hold us all together in a single project. It was like staring into empty space.

But it was a space we should not have to face just yet. Every day was the same. Early parade in the half-dark, after hasty wash and dress; breakfast; back in the hut to polish boots and badge; strip and barrack the bed, folding blankets and sheets into a short of sandwich; sweep and dust our own space, taking turns to clean the stove and hearth, ready for hut inspection before parading down the steep track to work. Our personal aims had gone grey. All the colours had faded away.

Mrs Lang was promoted to a senior rank, senior commander, and now sported a crown on her shoulder. There was by this time another kine detachment at Weybourne, on the north Norfolk coast.

We kines had flourished and multiplied.

April had come, but had come unnoticed. We had had mizzly weather for longer than was endurable. Everything was damp. We were used to the Nissen hut running with condensation; Honor was used to sleeping with a groundsheet over her blankets because the only ventilation was the door next to her bed; we were used to drying our damp blankets round the stove in the evenings; but this spell had depressed us more than usual. Damp crept into our boots; towels became clammy; there was mould inside our very barrack boxes.

Before I opened my eyes on this particular morning, the first thought, as always, was to get hold of my cold, damp clothes and get them into bed to warm them, before getting out of my warm, damp pyjamas. Then I realized what day it was. My birthday. My twenty-third birthday. Old! Where had my youth gone? Nothing of any importance had yet happened to me. Life had passed me by. Here I was, in this cold, miserable place, with another day of standing by, doing nothing, behind me and before me.

What had my life been, up to now? Twenty years – twenty-one years, to make a teacher of me. Well, that had been a waste of time. But at least there had been things to learn, some effort. Then the first year in the Army. New skills, new friends, more effort. But this last year? No progress, nothing new, no achievement. No lover, no hint of anything that might lead to marriage, no nothing. Nothing but a succession of grey days, dank and smelling of wet wool.

'Come on, girls, PYT! PT outside today. Wakey, wakey! Up!'

Groan. It's Beth. She's let that stripe of hers go to her head. Outside? She's mad.

Suddenly I was wide awake. Four monsters round my bed.

'Someone has to be bumped!'

They took hold of me, one to each limb, dragged me to the space between the beds, and up I went, and down I came ...

'One!'

And again ...

'Two!'

Do people still get bumped on their birthdays? Nowadays it sounds like part of the barbaric past. A strange, wild, loving, nerve-testing, friendship-bonding, foolish custom. But it beats birthday cards. And you know who your friends are.

'Twenty-two! Twenty three!'

And not a single bruise.

It was only after this that it came to me that the sun was shining. It was a lovely, sweet, bright day. The sun was actually shining on us, straight down the middle of the hut. It was Saturday. Only half-day working, and there might be some work; then a planned visit to Milford Haven, where there was to be an art-and-craft exhibition.

Later that morning, I was, unusually, at 'A' Station, on the Manorbier cliff, surrounded by bluebells and wonderfully fragrant gorse, with Peggy Welch leading the other two in a birthday song for me:

Angel eyes saw you, angel voices drew me to you ...
Dearly beloved, how clearly I see
Somewhere in Heaven you were fashioned for me ...

And the sun blazed down, the damp evaporated out of our clothes and out of our spirits, and the fact that I was old melted away.

In all the years since, no birthday has ever made me feel so old again.

The day fulfilled its promise: we managed to scramble into service dress and the transport for that unique trip to Pembroke Dock and the ferry across the Haven. Blue sea, blue sky and friends to enjoy it all with. On the ferry we ate the picnic that Xenia had prepared for us, chugging past the great flying-boats and among the screaming gulls.

'Do you mind if I don't come out tonight? I've got a bit of a headache.'

'But it's Saturday!'

Honor was beginning to have trouble with her eyes. The headaches were getting worse. Our work was hardly what the doctor ordered, spending all the bright sunny hours staring into the sky, mostly through a telescope, and then coming indoors, using the dark evenings to peer into the poorly lit evaluator at faint white marks on grey film, trying to read off the scales accurately and quickly.

On Monday she attended sick parade. The MO said she couldn't go on doing the work we were doing. It would damage her eyes, so it would be a good thing to re-muster into a different trade, immediately. She protested: surely there were duties that she could do and remain in kines? A compromise was reached. Practice camp work was not so exacting, and there was a vacancy at Bude. And, in the way that the Army has, it all took place in a few days.

Sadly we said our *au revoirs*, and she went. An important chapter of my life was over with her going. We kept in touch, of course, and remained friends, but nothing could replace that constant daily contact. And although we had never been sentimental towards each other – far from it – we missed each other badly. I still had Winn, of course, and Rita and Verona and the others; and barrack life and the mess room and the dances and the cinema outings and supper at the shop; and the work carried on. But it was different.

The war was moving on. The Axis Powers had been driven right out of Africa by now, and things were happening at last. The pace was hotting up.

During the long-drawn-out winter it had been the damp that had begun to play me up. My hand – my drawing hand – began to feel rheumaticky and was not always steady. A slight restlessness began to take hold of me. Mrs Lang sent for me. She offered me promotion!

There is no need to dwell on my brief career as a lance-corporal. The stripe had hardly been wetted; I had hardly learned the NCO gesture (breathe on the fingernails and rub the left sleeve) when Val came rushing into our hut, with news.

'I spy strangers!' we all howled.

'No – listen – I've got a secret! Gather round, you lucky little auxiliaries, and listen to Auntie.'

It seemed that her date from the previous night had let slip that a new practice camp was proposed for Clacton.

'Clacton?'

'Don't be daft, Val. They'd never do practice firing from there.'

Clacton, on the most exposed part of the Essex coast, was right on the bombing flight path from Europe to London. Surely there must still be some safer places that could be used. But Clacton! If it were true – if it were possible – fifty miles from Romford, on a direct rail line. It would be possible for me to get home for weekends. Oh!

Rita looked interested, too. Her father was still living at Croydon, and Kathleen and Joan at Pinner, and Winn at Southend.

'We'll have to start applying now. There'll be lots who want it.'

'But how can we? You can't apply for something you're not supposed to know about.'

'We don't even know if it's true. Who told you, Val?'

'Oh, unimpeachable sources, I do assure you. It's pukka gen.'

RAF slang. Who had told her?

After some thought, we found a formula:

To the OC 6th KT Detachment

Ma'am,
In the event of a practice camp ever being opened on the Essex coast: Clacton, for instance, may I be considered for a posting to the kine detachment?
[Having the honour to be, of course, her humble and obedient servant.]

To none of our letters was there a hint of a response.

Life went on as usual. Spring had truly come, and the beauty of the place started its seductions again. There was not so much standing-by, in the better weather. In the week, kine stations and gun-park romances, walks to the village and walks on the cliffs.

Being a local/acting/paid lance-corporal did not make much difference to my life. Apart from having to assemble the early morning parade sometimes, being called 'duty NCO' instead of 'duty orderly' on fire picquet, and taking turns with Beth to say 'Shun!' for kit inspections, life was not much changed.

There had been one or two changes in the detachment. Kathleen's sister Joan had waited to be called up from her

Civil Service job before joining us. Conscription for young women had come in, and it was only sensible not to volunteer. Conscripts had their money made up by the government.

Joan was not at all like giggly Kathleen. Beth, Kath Davies and Kathleen were all middle children of three, and we invented the theory that that position gives a sweet nature, easy-going and cheerful. And here was the elder sister. She was tall, taller even than Verona, and she was slow of speech and slow to smile. But her apparently straight face would slip sometimes, and she would drawl some penetrating comment that had us all in stitches. Heather's sister Rosemary also came to join us. Sally Atkinson and Molly Atkinson, and one or two more.

Molly was from a farm in Yorkshire, and when her family killed a pig, there was great rejoicing at Lydstep. Parcels of wonderful delicacies arrived, and we gorged ourselves on sausages and brawn, pâtés and cured tongue and pies.

A notice went up in Part I Orders: 'The following personnel are posted to the AA Practice Camp at Clacton, w.e.f. – [one day very soon] – Cox, V., Bates, M., Goldson, W., Bruce, I., Jepson, D.'

So, it was true about Clacton. True!

But not Brewer, D. It wasn't fair. Hadn't I been the one who thought up the way to apply? I bravely bearded the lion in her den.

'But you must understand, Brewer, that you would have to lose your stripe. It is only a local appointment.'

I managed to convince her that I wanted the posting more than the stripe. My mother was getting better: after seventeen months she was healing, but it was still an anxiety to me.

It was impossible, it seemed, to send me with the first contingent, but she promised to consider me, if I was resolved to give up promotion etc etc, responsibility etc etc, for inclusion in any other party that might be called for, at any time. So it was that Winn, on her arrival, bagged a bedroom for two, reserving the other bed for me.

The posting did come through.

But – to leave Lydstep! Goodbye to the bay, goodbye to

the gully, goodbye to Mrs Walters, to the Dak, to 'Mrs Bay
Leaf' in Tenby, with her sea-fresh fish teas, to the cliff
walks, the wild flowers, Lydstep House and the wood,
Major Mac and the trial that would never end. The walk
across the dunes to Penally, with its newly discovered
sand roses; the headland, where my house was going to
be built one day, in my fantasy. Goodbye to the jolly
crowd of permanent staff sergeants who had been such
good friends to our little group; and goodbye to
barrack-hut life and the damp mists and the pearly sea,
fishing for mackerel and watching for oyster-catchers.
How could I leave the place?

Val's posting had been delayed, for some reason, and
one day early in August we travelled together to London.
Oh, the luxury of a day-time journey!

We were settling ourselves down in our third-class
carriage, preparing to open our picnic, when a familiar
face went past. It stopped and came back to look at us.

'My wonderful ATS!' It was Renée Houston, a favourite
comedienne of the time. She opened our carriage door,
saying, 'I simply must give you lunch. Will you let me?'

Her presence was overwhelming. The make-up, the
perfume, the vigour, the aura. She would not be denied.
('This could only happen in wartime,' we giggled to each
other.) She marshalled us into the dining-car, sat us down
at a table near her own and ordered the best of the menu
for us. She waved and called to us throughout the meal,
until the whole of the embarrassed company of English
first-class railway passengers finally let their faces crack,
and smiled, and even spoke. Her high spirits were
infectious; and the lunch was very good.

'I'll collect the eggs.'

The first morning of my leave. It is the best moment of
all. And this was a particularly good one. August, no air
raids, civvy clothes and home.

Collecting the hens' eggs is supposed to be the nicest
job of all. Chickens lay in the warm nest boxes, and all you
have to do is lift the lid, and there you are. Not these
fowls. They had been raised by a broody duck, who had
long since passed away, and these orphans, who had not

spoken to a duck since they were a few weeks old, laid their eggs anywhere and rolled them in the mud. Why was it always our animals that were crazy? There is only one thing to be said in defence of the true mud-rollers: ducks are absolutely regular in their egg-laying habits; and if there are four ducks, there will be four eggs every day for a hundred days, when suddenly there will be none, till next year. So you know how many you are looking for. Chickens are different. If there is a cock-eyed way of doing something, a chicken will find it. So here I was, searching in muddy corners, being careful where I trod, looking for an uncertain number of eggs.

We breakfasted sumptuously, celebrating my posting and my home-coming. We laughed a bit: too much, perhaps, trying to forget the previous evening. I had arrived home late, and Daddy had already gone to work. There was a curious smell in the house. An aroma of boiling bacon, and something else. Mummy said, 'I hope you can be brave. Don't go into the kitchen just yet.' She brought me some tea in the living-room and explained. We did not play the 'Good news first, or bad news?' game in those days. It all came out at once.

She had been lucky enough to have been given some bacon bones at the small provisions shop. (It was illegal to sell bones, and no one ever saw one, normally.) The Co-op had had a stock of Kilner jars, and Daddy had gone down with his wheelbarrow and bought some. The Ministry of Food had instructed people never to try to preserve meat. It could be very dangerous. But she thought: what about the potted tongue you could buy in jars? That was preserved in a vacuum. But it was always packed in jelly. *Ergo* ... So there was a pot of bacon bones now boiling on the stove in the scullery, and Daddy had killed six rabbits before going out. He had gutted them but not had time to skin them. (He had killed them himself? He always got old Wybrow to do it for him.)

'Can you be very brave, dear? He did so want to have it all out of the way before you came home. I'd do it myself, but my silly wrist isn't strong enough.'

The six rabbits were hanging up above the Cookanheat stove in the kitchen, still warm. My parents wanted to spare me the shock of rigor, on top of everything else.

My mother had seen them born, fed them and stroked them. Next winter they would make twelve dinners. She gave me the knife my father had sharpened ready and told me what to do. It is easy, really. Just that you can't think about it.

The newspapers were full of sketch maps that week, with arrows arching and squiggling all over them. Churchill had made his speech about the 'soft underbelly of Europe', and the invasion of Italy had begun. Sicily had been a triumph, and now the Allied forces had established a good beach-head in Anzio. Now things would really start fizzing. A month or two to clear the enemy out of Italy, and then the real Invasion would take place. Over by Christmas? But we had said this so many times.

It was my last day of leave. A precious day in town. The shop assistant was very patient with me. That was nothing unusual: shop assistants were expected to be patient. I was in Harrod's, buying a pair of kid gloves. Wartime austerity regulations had their advantages, here and there: I should not have been doing this, in normal times, but the very fact of shortages had opened up the very expensive shops to people like me who did not want to spend too much money on clothes.

The whole national effort was now geared to 'essential' production, for the war machine. Blankets, towels, saucepans and beds were being produced on a very narrow range of designs, durable and dull, and were available only for the newly married, who were issued with their dockets along with the marriage lines. Clothes and fabrics were not only rationed: they too were subject to the tighter restrictions. Factories had to turn out a certain proportion of Utility goods, marked with the CC41 mark and sold under a certain price; and shops had to stock them. *Haute couture* was out: even the very wealthy were now affected by the war. It was these wartime rules that began to close the very wide gulf that existed not so much between the poor and the comfortable as between the comfortable (if reasonably economical) and the wealthy.

The range of clothes prices before the war was, in

proportion, much wider than nowadays. There was not the middle range of 'designer' clothes that we see, off the peg, nowadays. More women could sew and could make a summer dress from good-quality cotton prints, for less than 2 shillings, and if a dressmaker made it instead, say 3 shillings. Jap silk could be bought in the market for 3 pence a yard. It was not durable, but who wanted to wear a party dress a second time? Sensible spun silk, for blouses and underwear, was not much dearer, only the better-quality beautiful silks costing more than 2 shillings or so. And a good dressmaker would make it up to fit perfectly for a few shillings, or more, depending on the details.

Ready-made ladies' clothes were cheap and shoddy in the emerging chain stores, durable but frumpish in the Co-op, dearer in the department stores ('Can Ay help you, Modom?'). Not very stylish, but well finished. The gown shops guaranteed exclusivity, and for 2 to 3 guineas, for a very special occasion, a model could be bought. (The models were the clothes; the girls were called 'mannequins'.)

Men, of course, had their suits made to measure. Towns were as full of 'bespoke' tailors' shops then as there are shoe shops nowadays. Prices were anything from about £5 to £10 or so, but in recent years men had had another alternative, as well as the ready-made coarse working clothes that were very cheap. A firm calling itself the 'Fifty Shilling Tailors' had devised a sizing system, whereby dozens of half-finished garments hung in view, waiting to be tried on; and a very good approximate fit could be got by individual finishing.

But between these high-street shops and the luxury trade of Savile Row and Bond Street there was very little available. Couturiers could charge up to £100 for something rather nice, and there was nothing much below £50. Only for the rich.

And now, by wartime decree, the whole picture changed. No women's dress or suit or coat was allowed to cost more than £20. I am not saying that we all rushed to Dior and snapped up all the bargains, for £20 was still a lot to spend on a dress, but it brought things into some sort of proportion.

The Utility mark applied to everything: underwear, gloves and shoes. A pair of Utility gloves must not cost more than £1. And all shops were obliged to stock them, if they wished to sell their more expensive wares. It was wonderful, shopping in the best stores, in wartime. I spent a very happy half-hour in Harrod's, that day, choosing my pair of Utility gloves. It was a real ritual, in those days, with Modom drooping her dainty hand over the velvet wrist-support on the counter, being fitted by the well-disciplined assistant. Harrod's, of course, were incapable of selling cheap leather. These were beautiful.

Millinery was still not controlled. That day there was a frivolous little bit of nonsense for sale at 20 guineas.

Another pleasant wartime regulation said that remnants of cloth could be sold at half-coupon rate. Liberty's was a godsend to its faithful customers. If you searched long enough, moving to all the tables on the landings, often three or even four identical 'remnants' could be found. Plenty for a dress, in the abbreviated wartime fashions.

War is not all bad. Nearly all, but not quite. Some good comes out of it. Stiffening the sinews does not always lead to killing someone; summoning up the blood is not always for destruction.

Politicians found that they could work together, if need be; and those other old rivalries, of the medical and scientific worlds, dissolved into co-operation. Most of the world-changing discoveries of the present century were developed during those years.

But the greatest change that took place was in the role of women. Not the vociferous minority, who had knocked the men's head together and won the franchise, but the common lives of ordinary women. The nation had needed all the hands it could get. Women came out of domestic service into another kind of uniform, or they went into factories, making munitions – and more money than they had seen in all their lives. This meant that the going rate for housework, ordinary charring, began to go up. Charwomen were asking, and getting, half-a-crown an hour!

Ivy had been coming to us since we first lived in

Romford; a new friend of my mother's had recommended her. She was head mistress of 'the MD school', as it was known in the thirties, and she had picked out Ivy, at fourteen years old, as a good houseworker for herself but did not want her all the week.

'You'll find her clean and honest,' said Mrs Crossley, 'and hungry. Give her 1s. 6d. a day and as much food as she can eat.' So Ivy divided her week between the two households.

My dad said, 'One-and-six a day? That's monstrous!' and gave her half-a-crown.

Ivy was delighted. She was all that Mrs Crossley had said, and more. She was hard-working, and you could trust her to do the washing-up. There was no washing or ironing for her to do: my mother must have had the first washing-machine and ironer to come out of Canada. She liked using them herself.

In 1944, when Ivy was about twenty-seven years old and she had not been conscripted, probably because she would not have passed a medical board, it was obvious that her wages ought to go up. She was very well pleased to come to a house with plenty of eggs and plenty of milk, and she was fond of my mother, too. But she could have got a job anywhere, doing what she was best at. Her only fault was that she was completely unadaptable. She made up her mind what to do each day, and did it. If you tried to change what she had planned, she would put on her hat again and go home.

'I can't stay, Mrs Brewer. You've flummoxed me. I'll have to go home.'

If Ivy had decided to 'do out' the pantry and you had a friend coming to tea, it was just too bad. Ivy would go on finding more and more terrible things to bring into the daylight as the afternoon wore on. She would burst into the living-room with a dripping bag or a leaking tin: 'What do you want me to do with this one, Mrs Brewer?'

But what we should have done without her when my mother came home still an invalid, I do not know. Even if I had come home, I could not have managed as she did.

Yet even Ivy, with her leaden complexion and high-pitched giggle, did find something better to do than charring, later on. The days of the baby-sitter were approaching, and Ivy had an easier life ahead. And later still, she was destined for the only worthwhile career for any woman, however ambitious and capable. She had a young man, and they were to be married.

10 'Owing to the Death of the Luftwaffe ...'

Clacton, Summer 1943 to Summer 1944

Clacton proved to be another world. After the soft Welsh air, dimmed in mist and damp, here we had bright, stimulating east coast sharpness. And after the atmosphere of Trials Wing, with its sense of academe – academe in Arcadia, it was too abrupt a change, to come to this rustling, bustling town. No wild, craggy clifftops here. No flower-strewn bays with rare sea birds. Here was a straight shoreline, flat and barbed-wired, fronting the grey North Sea for four level miles.

Our quarters were in a requisitioned boarding-house. Other ATS were in the rest of the short street, and a sentry (male) was sitting on guard at the top of the road, and another at the foot. Winn had chosen for us a little room at the top of the house, with a sideways look at the sea. We talked long into that first night.

Traffic noises woke me, and the smell. Through the street smell of diesel and gas and dust, a sharper scent: the cold seaweed smell of the North Sea. Pavements and pollarded plane trees, and a built-up promenade along the shore. This was my natural habitat; but I had lived that other life so long that it made me sad.

There was no time for that. My bicycle had not yet arrived, and a corporal – Isobel Bruce from Lydstep: 'Hullo!' – put her head into our room.

'Gun-park this morning. Transport outside here, 8.45. Be there.' No instructions about work.

Winn said, 'Don't worry. They'll tell us what to do. It's

125

mostly recording.'

The three-ton Scammel truck looked intimidating. Here there was no one to say, 'Get up in the front, Doffy.' Here were all strangers. How was I going to get up, clambering right up there?

The kines of this new detachment, which had been operating for about five or six weeks, were a different breed of kine.

'Hullo, I'm Pat Wadia.' She was not just pretty: she was elegant. How do you manage to look like that in battledress?

A different corporal came and checked my name on her list. She too was slim, her cap at a jaunty angle, her make-up impeccable, eyelashes and all, and perfumed to kill.

As it happened, no one in the truck was anyone I knew.

'What do I do today?' I asked.

'Oh, there's plenty of time to sort that out.'

'But ...'

'You'd better be a gun-simulator.'

Ah, that sounded more business-like. My word, that sounded rather grand! Gun simulator! Mmm.

I tried to ask what it entailed, but my new colleagues were very busy planning a party that was to be held that night. Words such as *bouchées*, cocktail sticks, *vols-au-vent*, meringues, *canapés*, drifted around. I felt a bit out of my depth.

The corporal had not forgotten me. She handed me a large spanner in one hand, and a used shell-case in the other.

'It's fuze-prediction tests. When the fuze-setter says, "Fire!" count 1 2 3 4 5; then bang them together.'

Gun-simulator. Well, it served me right, and my heart yearned for Major Mac.

This was a practice camp, and a big one. From Jaywick in the west to Holland-on-sea in the east, for three miles along the entire length of the promenade, anti-aircraft guns paraded side by side, staring out to sea, into the sun. Heavies on the extreme right, as far as the pier; then Bofors units, from the pier to the 'cliffs' of Holland. After

Manorbier we had to laugh: these cliffs were five feet high. A small mine-field intervened, then there was an open space, occupied by Americans. American Army Air Force, with Browning guns. The guns for the 'tail-end Charlies' in their Flying Fortresses. It was here that our 'B' Station was.

No kine-theodolite, however; only an old Vickers predictor. This was indeed a come-down. But good news and bad news: no film to load, develop and evaluate, but lots and lots of computing, from lots and lots of readings. There were twelve regiments in, at any one time. They could have used ten times our number: we were wanted everywhere.

Lorna Parkes was our officer here. Some of us remembered her as our AI kine, at Manorbier. She was very good at saying 'No' to commanding officers who wanted us to work all the hours of the day and night.

The weather remained fine. There was always a target, plane and drogue, poodling up and down, right to left, then left to right, against a grey sky or a blue sky or a threatening sky. Up and down, above the straight parallel lines of beach, breakers and horizon. Flat. Everything was flat. All the morning, all the afternoon and most of the long, double-summer-time evening.

Boom, boom, boom. Pop-pop-pop-pop. Crack-crack-crack-crack-crack. First the heavies, then the light, then the machine-guns. And vice versa, coming back. Target, sleeve, observe!

One day Winn and I were to go to 'A' Station for a change. Turn right, along the front. Past the pier. On our left as we rode by the interminable row of guns, the shouting as they were brought into action and the generators being started up. The old hotels on the other side of the road looked sad, as if missing the laughter of past days.

We pedalled through the gates of Butlin's holiday camp, which hogs the next half-mile or so of coast line. 'There's the NAAFI.' The faded notice still proclaimed it 'The Venetian Ballroom'. We pedalled round the dry swimming-pool, the blue paint of its superstructure peeling in the parched air. Past the chalets and the mess halls. Here were the quarters of the permanent staff.

At last, the old golf course, flat, of course, like everything else here. Trampled and dusty, crowded with instruments and gunners, loud with the shouts of NCOs. I had been here before. We threaded our way through the hundreds of predictors and came to the kine post. Another old Vickers predictor. Isobel greeted us: 'You can go and put the kettle on.'

Our 'rest room' was one of the Jaywick houses. The whole estate lay derelict and pathetic. No one had been allowed to come and patch the matchwood walls, the insubstantial roofs, and to keep the ways clear. The sand had taken over. Bleached concrete roadways and dry, pale, blown sand. But the kines had found a reasonably solid chalet bungalow, and here was all the familiar brewing-up and frying-up equipment. Perhaps it was not going to be too strange. There was an Aladdin oil stove, some cans of paraffin, and the water had been turned on.

'They put a new lock on the door and cleared the place out, so that we should have a loo we could use. But we've improved the place a bit.'

There was coal still in the bunker, and a fireplace to use it in. Winn lit the oil stove, and I filled the kettle. In a cupboard were the tea, the tinned milk and some sugar. We put everything out, ready for break-time.

Things were not altogether changed. The Army was still the Army, and kines were still kines. And there was still plenty more that could be done with the house.

We worked long hours at Clacton all the week, but they played fair with us: weekends were free, after midday on Saturdays. The admin. tried to order us on church parade on Sunday mornings, but someone must have interceded for us, and we were free to go home for weekends.

It may have been due partly to Val Cox. When we had been ordered to declare our 'religion', most of us were the usual 'when in doubt, C of E'; being anything else does not excuse you church parade – you just stand at ease outside the church till the end of the service. But Val thought it was worth a try. We thought up twenty-two different Christian or near-Christian sects for us all to be, one for each of us.

It may have been Val's idea that did the trick.

Of course, we managed to enjoy life at Clacton. There were trips to Colchester, to the repertory theatre, to the evening classes where we tried to learn the Morse code; and all the weekends at home.

The war was making slow and painful progress. Italy was proving harder than expected. It did not augur well for that other invasion which was awaited so impatiently. But we bashed on with our work, recording height-finder tests and fuze-prediction tests and using our funny old predictors at stations, instead of kines. The Americans at Holland-on-Sea were very anxious that we should try their Browning gun. It is an odd sensation, standing in the middle of the ring, swinging the gun round you. It spits, its fire very rapid. By the time I had got used to it and tried to aim at the target flag, the pilot had decided to go home. Now why did I get the blame for that?

It was decided to give us all a sort of extended long weekend for Christmas. Never was a decision more welcome. We were tired; we needed the break. My mother was stronger every day; she had made a complete recovery. Thank goodness, though, she had given up trying to go back to her air-raid warden's job. Even she admitted that things were not so desperate now. She had taken up lace-making – pillow lace. There were no air raids; all that work in the garden was paying off, and the food shortages did not affect my parents as much as some. The animals were better organized, the apples were stored, the plums all bottled, Bessie had got her act together and was now in full milk production, and altogether it was a breathing-space.

Back, after Christmas, to Clacton's hard, ever harder winter. The days were bright, and day after day the practising went on. It hardly ever rained. We could see the clouds gather over the sea and watch them sail over us and drop their rain over the village of Great Clacton, a mile inland. No respite. No standing-by.

It grew colder. The east wind was like a knife. Riding our bikes along the front, our faces were numb before we reached the gun-park. It was a question of heaping on as many clothes as possible. Layers of underwear, two pullovers, the battletop, greatcoat and leather jerkin on top of that; big, winding scarf, and 'spanker' gloves. It is a wonder we could walk, let alone mount and ride a bicycle. Sometimes the wind would moderate a bit, and in the sunshine the recording work could be almost enjoyable. The working day was long, and the recording instruments varied. The gunners were now competent at their drills, hits were commonplace and near-misses usual.

The job I liked best was lying at full stretch in the spotter's chair: that wonderful contraption, a canvas chair with movable arms, a headrest and mounted on a swivel. With a pair of binoculars and a partner to write down your assessment of each burst, it really was the life. Great fun. And if a friendly gun team gave you a hot shell straight from the gun, from time to time, to put under the lap-rug, it was almost comfortable. But it was not always like that, and mostly we came back to quarters shuddering with cold. We were no more popular with the admin. than we had ever been; they found us a nuisance with our funny working hours.

On one particularly cold day, when we came back frozen and in need of soup or fried cheese, baked beans or potato patties, which the cook made quite well, we lined up for our tea. We stood there in the queue, each thumping the back of the one before us. (There is no better way of being warmed up when you are thoroughly chilled.)

The hatch was flung up: 'Oh, it's you lot. You decided to come for tea, then.'

And what were we given? Cold spam. And a special treat – goodness knows where they had come from – half a raw tomato. Cold. We all broke down and cried.

We were not the only ones who were tired and cold and dispirited. The nation was at full stretch, and the effects were beginning to show. Families can stand being separated for so long; coming home each day to a hundred kinds of discomfort can be borne for so long. People were getting tired of the war. Nothing happening, no encouragement. Everything took time. Getting a meal, queuing for fish, the only unrationed food; rations of fats and tea and sugar had to be bought in tiny little scraps. The Min. of Food advised us what to do: eggless cakes and sugarless cakes, fatless cakes using liquid paraffin, carrot cakes. To cook the little bit of bacon so carefully, not to waste a scrap of it. All these things took time. No spitting beefsteak, cooked in a moment and brought straight to the table. Meat was much too precious to use like that. It was all so tiring.

Fear makes you tired, as well as pain; being unhappily parted from those you love makes you tired. Having no time for silly little pleasures is dispiriting. Digging for Victory. Travelling to work in slow, infrequent trains. It all robs you of your life. And people were beginning to ask: 'What's it all for? What about this Western Offensive?' 'Give Hitler a bloody nose at Dunkirk,' some said. Hitler was still the enemy, not the ordinary German people. Gunners who said, 'There's no such a thing as a good German!' and 'The only good German's a dead German,' were shouted down, No, no. Hitler had misled them.

Love your enemy? It is true that every Sunday we were told to try. But at least we were being taught, all the rest of the week, to laugh at him. Perfect love casts away fear, and laughter drives away fear, too. To this day we are still, on television, watching films that were made at that time, and we have learned to laugh in a different way. Not at the old image but at our own attitudes, so many years ago.

It wasn't only the enemy we laughed at. The old Venetian Ballroom of Butlin's holiday camp was the gunners' NAAFI. It was palatial in size, the floor was not completely ruined, the ceiling was a triumph of lighting design, and two walls, butting to a corner, were made of floor-to-ceiling mirror – twenty foot long to the corner, and as much along the side. Some wag had caused to be printed, in foot-high letters, all along the top: 'TAKE A LOOK AT YOURSELF. ARE YOU A CREDIT TO YOUR UNIT?'

Most of us had added to our worktime outfit a balaclava helmet, and we truly were a sight to see.

The detachment naturally divided itself into two parts: those who went home for the weekend, and those who didn't. We who did were very pleased to do so: after all, that was why we had asked to come here. But those whose homes were too far away made themselves a very adequate social life, and they were having a whale of a time. So, all things considered, we were a fairly contented group. The fly in the ointment was our old enemy: not enough hot water to wash in.

The GD officer told Lorna plainly: 'We can have only one boiler repaired in The Croft. I'll have to have my girls' part of the house done. I know your kines: if they want anything enough, they'll get it somehow.'

'Bloomin' cheek!' we said, when we were told.

And here, once more, we experienced another sort of kindness. The WVS came to our rescue. They found enough of their members and friends to let one of us use the bath in their home, once a week. Some even offered two. The bank manager's wife gave Tuesday evenings to Rita and me, and we spent a few pleasant hours in the very sumptuous flat above the bank, being treated like human beings.

It was January 1944. Our work was necessary, no doubt, but repetitive and dull. Winn and I began to be homesick for Lydstep. Spring would be stirring there already. Whatever had we left the place for? There was one advantage of going home at weekends: it meant that parents would not mind so much if you spent a leave somewhere else.

The cliffs called us. Those cliffs that so terrified me to scramble along, I craved for. The spring flowers, the soft air, Caldy, Mrs Walters, Major Mac. I'd love to see him again. And old friends, still in the detachment. We decided to spend our next leave in Tenby. We booked ourselves into one of the little houses that stand along the quay that encloses the harbour there.

So on 7 February we caught the old, familiar train. Nine o'clock in the evening at Paddington. You had to be there at eight, to be sure of getting a seat, and we had plenty of time to settle and to remind ourselves of the old, familiar scenes.

It was a matter of honour – of female honour – to get there early. We were not going to be like a certain type of helpless-looking female we utterly despised. At two minutes to nine, there would always be one little old lady who would arrive just in time to catch the train, but all the seats would have been taken up long ago. The dear, sweet thing would climb into the carriage, look at her (very heavy) baggage on the platform, look round at all the big, strong soldiers who were preparing, like everyone else, for an all-night journey and expect one of them not only to get her luggage and stow it but to give up his seat as well. And one of them always did. It made us savage. It was not fair. In those days men always treated women as ladies. It was taken for granted. Therefore it was up to a woman to behave like a lady and play fair. But many did not. There was such a one this time. We made a point of not answering her soppy questions about the awful time we must be having; we went to sleep.

Night trains did not take the short route through the tunnel: they went all round Gloucester way. It was almost completely dark in the carriage, and airless with the blinds drawn down. The familiar crowded train, the smell of khaki, baggage piled up everywhere; and when the engine came to the hilly bits and nearly gave up, we knew we were in Wales. The backing and shunting woke everybody up, and there were the usual sarcastic remarks about the railway and about Wales:

'When it starts to go a bit faster,' we said, 'it's only to get up enough steam to put the brakes on.' Forward, then backward for a mile or two, then lots of shudderings, then forward again. And we could see none of this: we were blacked out.

The taxi took us to the house, and Mrs Williams welcomed us in. But we could hardly bear to go inside, at first. The fresh morning, the harbour wall, bright in the sunlight. Gulls on the wall, waiting to be fed. 'Even the gulls grow bigger here,' we said, comparing them with the Clacton variety. She gave us Welsh cakes, among other things, for our breakfast.

Tenby. The sunlight was not the hard brightness of the east coast but a sweet light, bathing the cobbles and stones of the old walls into warmth. Winn and I made our pilgrimage. We drank our fill. Tenby first, then the bus to Manorbier Bay, where the last of the snowdrops we found in the valley, near the old dove-cote. Primroses everywhere. The long climb up to the church, with the grass of its steep churchyard short now that it was winter, the tombstones leaning this way and that, peaceful in the sunshine. Gulls overhead and the sea a bit restless today, frothing on the rocks below us.

Lydstep next, of course. Old friends, and some new ones. Brenda Callingham; Aileen Sanders, whom I remembered from visits to 'B' Station, when she had been on the course; Gladys Tulett ('Tulip') who was now kine clerk, and she and Lois were now fast friends. Scottie was still there, and Heather, Chrissie, Mary Cowan and Verona.

If we were tired, we Clacton Practice Camp bods, the girls at Lydstep were dropping with fatigue. The work was accelerating, all at fever pitch. It was as though they knew something that we did not. Major Mac looked fagged out but greeted us with his old twinkle.

It was about now that there was better news from the Italian Front. After five months of bitter fighting, the deadlock broke. This could only bring the next stage one step further. But would we be ready for it? And, from the Enemy's point of view, now was the time for him to produce his 'secret weapon'. He would soon have to show his hand.

We went up the café with the gang that evening and waited for Mrs Walters to recognize us. Great rejoicing. And after the first ten minutes, it felt as though we had never been away. Those days that we spent down there took years off Winn. She was a new woman. The whole holiday was a great success. Some evenings we spent in the small harbour house in Tenby, our toes in the chimney corner, eating toast and fresh-made cakes, planning our days and talking. Once or twice it was the cinema, or a concert. Then off again next morning, to the sand dunes at Penally, or Lydstep again; and even, one day, over the cliffs to Saundersfoot, where the ferns were beginning to put up their curls, and the bluebell leaves were beginning to show. A bite and a drink in the pub, there on the beach. We felt very daring. But we were on holiday. Tenby again. The bookshops, the china shop.

Too soon it was time to say goodbye. And time to go back to the concrete seaside, in the town.

One thing was clear: requisitioned houses can be comfortable; having some personal privacy is civilized, and all very well when friendships have already been made; but in spite of all our grousing, there is nothing like the old barrack-room life. We had begun making new friends, in the space of a couple of days.

Back to Clacton, then, and the formalities of ATS routine.

Ten o'clock roll-call. Betty Goodfellow, duty corporal: 'Where's Jumbo?'

'She out on a date.'

'Damn her! She's late. That means I'll have to stay up till she comes in.'

This was different. Usually an absentee was ignored until morning, then put on a charge. But now, in this different atmosphere, we were waited up for.

Men were coming back from the Italian campaign, some with the Desert Rat flash on their shoulders. Battle-weary men, hard-faced in a way that we had not seen before. Military police were showing their presence more and more in the town. It was early spring, even in this arid, windswept place, and the pace of AA practice was accelerating. Instead of a month, batteries were coming in for only ten days, then off again. No time for the social niceties, no time for the slow introductions. 'Come out with me tonight?' They were demanding and impatient.

Jumbo came in late that night, giggling with embarrassment and shaken. The man who had taken her out had brought her back, unwillingly, to Penfold Road, which was out of bounds to the men, and from the end of the road had shouted after her: 'You cow! You old cow! You cheating, bloody cow! Lead a man up the garden, then cheat! Bloody old cow!'

Things had changed. It was quite frightening.

These men were tough. There were fights in the streets, and tension was everywhere. Two regiments of Royal Marines came in at the same time. The rivalry between them had become more than light-hearted banter, and they had to be kept apart. One was a battle-hardened regular regiment, newly returned from the Italian Front; the others were young recruits, with no war experience.

One response they had to each other was to maintain a smartness that was incredible, even for Marines. Their boast, to others than themselves, was that you could tell which regiment any man belonged to: one lot was half-an-inch taller than the other.

Into this new atmosphere Mrs Lang appeared again. Whether she stayed any length of time or not, I forget, but while she was with us, things began to happen. Plotting control was the great thing nowadays. The batteries have to practise, of course, banging away at a steadily moving target that patiently mooches up and down, obeying all the practice rules, but in real life there is a sky full of trouble, from which someone has to select a suitable target. We have all seen, in films, the plotting room: pretty young WAAFs dodging swiftly round the big, square plotting table, push model aircraft about with rakes, according to instructions received by telephonists on the balcony; and the plotting officer phones his squadron to give them their instructions. That was the old RAF method. But the new AA method was to have the radar information transmitted direct to the table, and moving lights indicated where the aircraft were. The game was to unravel something that could be engaged.

'Private Goldson! Brewer! Here's something up your street. How would you like to make up an air raid?'

In the real thing, gunnery instruments follow the bombers or their escorting fighters so that the courses can be transmitted onto the table. But the Army could not put on thousands of real aircraft, coming from all directions, twice a day for the next few weeks. It was up to us.

Winn and I copied on a large scale a map of the Essex coast, with ourselves as the Vulnerable Point in the middle of it, and filled it with courses of fictitious aircraft, plotted in time and space. We could start them off at different times, from different places, at different speeds: anything from 150 mph to 250 – even, in one case, 350 mph; some high, some low; some single aircraft, some in groups of 200 plus; mostly hostile, but some friendly, with the IFF code worked in; perhaps a lone slow one, losing height, supposedly a crippled bomber, one of ours, coming home after a raid on the enemy. We also allowed one or two to peter out altogether, and disappear. No, we were not simulating a hit: that was against the rules we were given. This was practice, not drama. The aircraft run that seemed to fizzle was the Germans' answer to our radar. The aircrews flung out of their bombers streamers made of aluminium foil, which floated down and bemused our radar: 'window-jamming'. We had a 'window' in each of the schemes we made up.

Then it was all hands to compute, working backwards. Instead of working from angles observed by the tracking instruments, in order to find a location and height, it was the other way round, every five seconds. Each pair of our girls had one target to simulate and a predictor in the plotting ante-room to feed it in. The room was crammed. There were permanent staff sergeants and AIGs and, at a table all by herself, the time-keeper. We all took turns at the various duties. It was only fair that we should have a turn at the worst one of all.

It is the most difficult job I have ever been called upon to do. It sounds nothing. It sounds easy, so easy, it is ridiculous. And yet I found it almost impossible. The schemes lasted twenty minutes. Someone had to call every five seconds, loud enough for the roomful to hear, her reading from a watch. That is all there is to it. If you don't believe me, try it. It gets harder and harder, and the last five minutes are sheer torture.

One day in May, we were all summoned into the computing-room. All recording duties were cancelled: this was an important meeting. The contingent from Manorbier managed to whisper some news: Joan Cotter was married. She was now Mrs (Dr) Hank Farrell, Jnr.

The brass – and, my word, there was some brass – sat at a table in the bay window. Mrs Lang presided, and each of the staff officers spoke to us in turn. The essence was this: every type of weapon-control dreamed up by man had been tried and practised; but the War Office considered that perhaps some obvious way of hitting an unseen aircraft had been overlooked. All the Great Brains of the War Office had been brought to bear on the subject, and a new thought had occurred to someone: why not throw the problem out to the little brains? And so they had come to us for help. Would we think about it and let them know if any bright ideas emerged?

Our response, as soon as they had gone, was immediate. After the bad language had subsided, Rita and I, in the space of a single evening, solved all their problems for them. Not one, but two new methods we devised.

Our report, entitled 'Lighter AA – New Methods of Unseen Fire Control for 40 mm AA', outlined two variations of each of two methods: Smethar and Magnar.

Smethar relied on the recently discovered fact that a special band of radio waves was sympathetic to 'Brylkreem', a hair preparation then widely used in the RAF, and was irritated by the *ersatz* Luftwaffe equivalent. The officer i/c drill was designated 000 – Offensive Odours Officer.

Magnar was a revolution in the whole philosophy of gunnery. Instead of the missile's being aimed to go to the target, the target was induced to be magnetized down to the gun; and in the refined version there was no need to fire at all.

We appended a list of equipment:

Headgear, degaussed	1
Cranes, headgear, degaussed	1
Pits, cranes, headgear, degaussed	1
Shovels, pits, cranes, headgear, degaussed	2

It was a detailed and complicated document, five typed pages long, accompanied by three pages of diagrams, with lots of lovely long words, most of which we had made up. It took us nearly a week to complete, and we sent it to the camp commandant. We had no direct answer from the CIG, the chief instructor of gunnery, but we heard that he had had copies made and was sending them, in the last IG's letter, to all practice and permanent staff units. We were so chuffed that we did not immediately notice what it was that we had been told.

Last letter?

A man with a secret, who says, 'Aha!' like Piglet, will soon have his secret wrested from him, but if he invents some implausible yarn, the wilder it is, the more likely it is, in times of uncertainty, to be believed. When, in June, the yellow-painted lines and numbers began appearing on the kerbs of the back streets of Clacton, we were told that,

a) a new drainage system was being put in the town;
b) a VIP was coming to visit, and these were the markers for an underground security listening network;
c) the whole camp was being moved, *en bloc*, and these were the M/T markers.

Everything happened so quickly that we did not have much time to argue about it.

One evening, when some of us were returning to quarters on a late pass, we noticed some of the towing vehicles with their generators parked around the town. Perhaps it was true: perhaps we were all going to be posted.

The next morning, something woke me early. It was not a noise. The sound of the sea, lapping the sea wall was all I could hear. The sound of the sea?

What had woken me was the silence. No engines, no shouting, no Army boots-at-the-double, no generators, only the sea. Winn was awake too, and together we rushed to the window and craned our necks out. Our little bit of foreshore was empty. During the night, while we had slept, they had gone. Twelve regiments of AA artillery, with their personnel trucks, all their cars, tiffy trucks, towing vehicles, generators, guns, the lot. Of course, that's what the yellow lines had been: assembly markers. We must have been stupid.

The town was empty. We cycled up to Butlin's, to see if anyone had any orders for us. Val, Rita, Pauline Ruizen, Peggy Adams, Kay Tuckey and I sat on the patch of grass in front of one of the chalets, opposite the plotting-room door.

The chalets, all in a row, each had a square grass plot in front, with a standard rose in the middle, a shrub rose on each corner, and a regimented rambler over the porch. Just the kind of place that the Army likes to keep tidy. It was June; and it really did make a pretty effect. These chalets were the permanent staff sergeants' quarters.

At ten o'clock we were still sitting on the grass, waiting for something to happen, when one of the young officers cycled by.

'Hullo,' he said. 'Why aren't you listening to the radio? It's just been announced. Allied forces have invaded Europe. In Normandy. Near a place called Caen, if that's how they say it. And it's going to be all right this time. The sergeants' mess – they're all drunk already.'

We lay back on the grass and stared at the sky.

'What's the date?' asked Peggy.

'5 – no, 6 June.'

'Well, they've got nice weather for it.'

'Nobody seems to want us. Let's go and find someone to celebrate with.'

Everyone had forgotten us. We were almost quiet for the rest of the day, trailing from radio to radio, in mess and quarters and café, in canteen and computing-room and milk bar.

It was a Tuesday. Winn and I had a friend, one of the PS sergeants, an Irishman. He was a married man, and he had started taking us out – both of us – for an evening walk, and a drink at the end of it, or to a café at St Osyth's. 'It's nice of him,' said Winn. 'He has a sense of decorum.' It was easy cycling distance, the café, and there were pleasant walks around. Double-summer-time in June. Long, long summer evenings.

'There's no more work for any of us here, you know. It's all finished. There'll be no more batteries coming in.'

'But what will they do with us?'

'As far as I know, they'll keep us all here, and occupy us with a few light duties, and lots of sport.'

Lorna called us to a meeting. We could go farming at Elmstead, if we liked. Fruit-picking, potato-picking, cabbage-planting.

That was the funniest one: sitting on the cabbage-planter, fitting the little plants into the forceps on a moving belt and watching them go round their little escalator ride and be poked into the ground. But I couldn't face this for what might be weeks, so Winn and I suggested a little local history search and were given permission.

There were messages from across the Channel, from the fighting front, in between our cycle rides and teas with vicars' wives. Some were too distressing to disturb now, but there was some good news. One communiqué began: 'Owing to the death of the Luftwaffe ...'

But that summer was not all cloudless. Exactly a week after D-Day, as we had come to call it, on the following Tuesday, 13 June, the first terror weapon was loosed on London.

I had laughed, on the day when the batteries had left, 'Whatever did I join up for? To do something about the defence of London, I thought. I should have gone to a mixed battery camp. Cupid's Cavalry. They're staying home to defend us. All this lot – as soon as they know their job, they're off abroad.'

But I was not laughing now. Here, then, it was. Attacks on London had begun again. Our friend told Winn and me that it was something new that was being used. He kept disappearing, then returning to Clacton to tell us about it. We thought of Trials Wing, preparing for something unknown and trying to be ready for it. But all too soon, we knew.

That first attack, on 13 June, was strange. No bombers had come in force, but something fell in Grove Road, Bow, in London's East End. We used to call it 'the road between the parks', because the end of it divides Victoria Park, near which a sister of my mother's lived. It was a big corner house, the street door giving straight onto the side pavement. It overlooked the park at the front, and a common at the side. Auntie Grace had been bombed out several times, and it had become almost a family joke. Her husband had his own small business and could not afford to leave the district. She was as possessive of the house as he of his firm, so they were a pair. We visited them often, and if they were not camping in what was left of the house, they were never far away.

Daddy heard that a plane had crashed with all its bombs in Grove Road, which ended very near them, so he called in on the way to work the next evening. They had had no damage this time, but they told him that it was the worst single incident they could remember. Grove Road had some very small houses, very close together, and there was more devastation and more lives were lost than in a whole night's bombing during the Blitz. The aircraft must have had its full load of bombs still on board. The odd thing was, there was no sign of it. Only some bits of twisted metal, and what might have been the fins of one of the bombs.

What nobody knew, and what the government made sure that nobody could know, was that this was the first of the pilotless bombs. The first of the Vengeance weapons. A flying bomb.

By Friday, more than seventy a day were reaching London. The whole population of a large city can't be made to believe that pilots are deliberately crashing their fully laden aircraft all over the place, and it had to be admitted by the Min. of Inf. that Hitler's terror weapon had been unleashed. On Saturday, when I got home for the weekend, it was in the newspapers. The buzz-bomb. The doodle-bug. Yes, that's right. Put a silly name on it, and it does not sound so terrifying.

But back in Clacton again, the world of AA was rejoicing. The so-long-looked-for terror was now made manifest. If you can see it, you can deal with it. And it could be dealt with. At last, here was every gunner's dream. A target on a constant course, at a constant height, at a constant speed. The classic. True, the speed was 400 mph (What?) but obeying all the rules. And now, with radar control, hits were inevitable. Those of us whose families were in London, even we, found ourselves joining in their infectious enthusiasm. Nearly all the male permanent staff left, to take part in the supervision of a big operation.

Half the AA units that were defending London were dispatched to locations along the south-east coast. At Southwold in Suffolk the Army had to make its own road to get the guns to the shore. It was all swiftly done, and very soon the robots had to fly through the coastal guns, then the RAF fighters, then the inner ring of guns and, last of all, the balloon barrage.

Success was phenomenal. Never had such an AA operation worked so well. But out of a total of nearly a hundred a day, some were bound to get through.

11 'Big Ben!'

St Margaret's Bay and Great Chart, Summer 1944 to Spring 1945

When Mrs Lang turned up again, we knew that things were bound to fizz. And we didn't feel like being fizzed. If there were to be postings, it could only mean Burrow Head, or Towyn, or Weybourne, or somewhere else miles from nowhere, and we had come to like being in the thick of things – and near home in time of trouble.

The brass was back, too. There we all sat once more, in our now unused computing-room, sarcastically waiting to be insulted again. But this time the atmosphere was different. This time they looked grave, and before anything else was said, they swore us to secrecy. Odd, that. Everyone in the room was bound by the Official Secrets Act, and by moral obligation.

'What you are about to be told,' the chairman said, 'is not to be breathed to anyone. The civilian population is having a hard enough time at the moment, without burdening them with something that might never happen.'

'Hitler's first secret weapon has now been revealed. We are dealing with that, and meeting with creditable success. The second one, you will be pleased to know, has been overrun by our invasion force; it was a great gun, but that will not now fire on London.'

London again! He did not look for applause or cheers, just went on looking grey.

'We have cause to believe that there is a third weapon. A very special rocket. There is an ambiguous reconnaissance photograph, which seems to show a rocket-like missile at one of the German factory sites. There is no corroboration;

and the whole of the Pas-de-Calais region has been meticulously photographed, but no sign of a launching-system can be detected.'

His colleague, on his left, held up a roughly drawn sketch of a child's rocket, just beginning to ignite.

'All we can hope for,' he said, 'is that, given the right conditions, a rocket when fired leaves a smoke trail. And if it is a large rocket, which this, if it exists, must be, that trail could be visible for several miles. It could be visible across the English Channel.'

He let that sink in for a bit, then said, 'Margaret.' Her excitement was well suppressed, but it was there all right.

'We have been asked,' she told us, 'to mount a watch from sites around the Kent coast. A constant day-and-night watch. If you find your name on the posting list, we hope that you will volunteer to do this duty. It is of very significant importance, and ...'

Olive Lane, our sergeant, stood up. 'Ma'am,' she said, 'we all volunteer, of course.'

The staff officers withdrew, and our CO gave us more details: 'It is envisaged that there will be four kine-theodolites, manned by a reinforced detachment, stationed, as you have heard, at places round the coast. Some of you will meet old friends again.'

She stood up to leave, and we all stood and crowded round Olive.

'I've been told to keep you here for half-an-hour to get it off your chests, then it'll be tea-time. There'll be a detail posted up tomorrow morning. Oh – and you'd better all start packing.'

We did not like rockets. Nasty, cheap, unpredictable things. A gun you could respect, but a rocket-launcher, such as we had seen at Manorbier, was more like a bit of Meccano that a demented child had thrown together than a proper gun, and the noisy missiles were wobbly and dangerous. Even we, fifty yards to the rear, were made to wear steel helmets when they were firing. And it looked as though some such dodgy bit of rubbish was the Führer's ultimate weapon.

'They're not even certain,' said Gina Porteous. 'They're not absolutely certain that the thing exists at all.'

'They're pretty sure. They must be.'

'Well, it's better than picking potatoes.'

In the event, it was decided to take a handful of us from all detachments and fill in as necessary. It was a complete shake-up of the kine world, and all were affected, one way or another.

My name was on the list, but not Winn's. It is possible that she had asked for a compassionate posting: I know that her father was not very well. She was sent to Sheerness, on the other side of the estuary from Southend, and a small RN ferry boat plied between Sheppey and Southend pier. She must have been pleased, though our parting was rather sad. 'But we shan't be too far away to visit.'

My Dad was pleased, when my letter home arrived. 'Now at last she'll have a bit of young life, and enjoy herself.' He could not stand the sight of Winn, for some reason. I could never take her home with me, after one disastrous visit.

St Margaret's Bay was fabulous. There is a sandy bay, but the road along the top of the cliff follows the outward curve of the South Foreland. To the left, looking out to sea, is Hope Point, with the coastguard station, and in front, between the road and the chalk cliff edge, a varying hundred yards or so away, stand several houses. Outside one of these the truck stopped, and we were told that here were our sleeping-quarters.

Gina said, 'Come on, Doffy!' and we raced up the stairs, to try to find a room with a sea view. 'This way!'

I followed her in, and sure enough it was a room that would please anyone. We began the usual 'bags I' for the window place, but there were two windows. One faced westward along the dip and sweep of the cliff to where the South Foreland lighthouse stood; the other was a dormer, looking straight across the Channel, just big enough to push a bed in. We did not have to toss up or bag; it was all too delightful. I pushed my bed into the dormer space, and she lined hers up with the other window. It looked over the walled fruit garden, and mine had the rose bed, still in bloom, in the middle of an overgrown lawn, which ended at the ungarded cliff edge. It was like a dream.

We could hear some happy reunions going on. Beth Sagar, Kath Davies and Kath Lavery were reunited and, together with Lois Howes, who had also appeared, were quartered with Mary Wilkin in the rooms – the chauffeur's rooms – over the garage of the house opposite. Ruth Rich was here, and Jessie Wareham, now a CSM. She, with Edna Heavisides, was in the room next to ours. (Edna had a twin, and they had never been separated before.) My heart missed a beat when I saw 'Welch' on the room list that Lois was making, but it was a girl called Lilian, not our Peg. Betty Wintersgill, too, from Lydstep. From Clacton, Verna Holliday, Joy Dalby and Isabel Bruce. The legendary Chris Purdy, every inch of her from Oxfordshire, a pre-war Territorial who had been called up at the very beginning and was on the first kine course. And a girl called Judy Garland.

We unpacked a bit, but the best was yet to see. Of the four or five houses along the seaward side of the road, this one, Hope Point, was ours; one was to be the men's quarters, one was for general duties ATS; and one was entirely for our working and recreation, and our officers' sleeping-quarters. 'Coggers', it was called. 'A real film star house,' we dubbed it, and then discovered that it *was*. George Arliss's. It was all curved windows, blue paintwork and black marble bathrooms. In the old drawing-room there was still the frieze of silhouettes of his friends, done straight on the blue wall, at their own natural heights. This room had an enormous bowed window. Above this there was a flat roof, with a French window into our CC post room. From up here Calais could be seen across the Channel, and the area we were to survey – or at least the sky above it. From the roof terrace at the side we could have seen all along the coast of the Dutch lowlands, if, as we said, the earth had been flat.

Lydsteppish, but not Lydstep. Restrained Lydstep, with luxury.

Daphne Cowper was our officer, remembered from Manorbier. She was a modest woman who ruled unobtrusively through her NCOs, and our extremely ordered life began very soon. There were two detachments at St Margaret's: forty-four of us. Half a detachment

– eleven – at Ramsgate and another half at Shorncliffe, near Folkestone. They each had a kine set up and housed, and they were quartered nearby. Here we had two: one up near the coastguard, and the other just along the cliff towards the South Foreland Light. Mrs. Lang presided over all proud that we were operational at last.

I was in the CC post squad and spent my watches in that very comfortable room, sheltered from any unkind wind. Incredible! Of course, we soon had a few chairs out on that terrace. There were, as might be supposed, four watches each twenty-four hours. Two of eight hours each, and two dog watches, of four. Three squads, therefore, move up one watch each day, so everyone gets a fair share of day and night duty.

We began. It was tough, but not too tough. At stations the team had three for watching, and one on the telephone. Of the three watching, while one was on her first ten minutes, the second was on her second, and the third was resting. Every ten minutes, move round one. A systematic search pattern was used, sweeping the whole of the Pas-de-Calais arc. We at CC post were ready to alert the other three kine stations, as soon as one had given the word. 'Fireworks!' was our code word. And if it should ever come to it, and we should have a target to follow and photograph, we were to log it as 'Big Ben'. Then, develop, evaluate, compute and phone the co-ordinates to RAF Manston, to bomb the site we had pinpointed.

After three weeks of nothing, I went on leave.

My parents and I visited Auntie Grace again. She was between laughing and crying. They had been bombed again. The tall windows lay smashed in the dining-room; the wooden shutters were awry. The front door was leaning up against the wall of the house; there was soot everywhere; the cat had kittens a fortnight old, and the dog had given birth that morning. A tin of red salmon had been opened to feed the cat, and luckily for the dog, the 'cat's meat man' was still operating. We tried to help where we could.

My aunt told us she had seen Aunt Alice that morning. My aged great-aunt, a single lady, who had been the unmarried one, kept at home. But Great-Grandma had been dead now nearly ten years, and Aunt Alice lived alone, in rooms. She had been invited to lunch and had arrived apologetically a little late. Stepping round piles of masonry in the gutters, having to avoid cordoned-off streets, had delayed her somewhat.

She tried to knock at the door, which was not in its place, so she called, 'Gracie!' She never would have walked in uninvited. Aunt Grace had gone to the door, a bit dishevelled and anxious, having forgotten all about the luncheon invitation. There was not much prospect of food, anyway, just yet.

'Oh, Aunt Alice! I'm so sorry. I'm afraid we're in a terrible mess. I couldn't let you know. Can we make it another day?'

'My dear Grace, don't give it another thought. If you can't manage it today, I'll come instead next week. Don't worry.' She put up her sunshade again, and turned back a moment. 'And you needn't be afraid. You know I never tittle-tattle about people's untidiness.'

And off she had gone. I was sorry not to have seen her.

We promised to take one of the puppies, when it was old enough, and a kitten, too, as soon as one of them could feed itself, when we noticed that one of the little creatures was eating some of the salmon! A fortnight old. So we took it home that day and discovered that, although it could eat, it couldn't lap, so we fed it with a dolly's feeding-bottle that I still had. That cat never did learn to lap with its tongue but put its face over a bowl of milk and slurped. We were quite pleased to have a cat again, and the promise of a puppy. Our two cats had died within a few days of each other, a year before; and our Donny, our sweet Samoyed Donny, had died at my mother's feet as she stepped indoors when she came home from Wycombe after her illness. He had missed me, always picking my letters out from the heap to bring into the kitchen; he moped when my father was at work, but he grieved for my mother when she was away, and stayed alive only long enough to greet her when she came home. I can still hardly bear to think about him.

When my leave was nearly over (it must have been 9

September), we heard, or read in the paper, that an enemy bomber, fully loaded, had crashed on a gas main in Chiswick and that it had caused unprecedented damage and casualties.

I was sure. I was sure that this was it. Why, oh why, did I have to be on leave? There were two more days still to go. It would be unthinkable to cut it short. I made some excuse to sit up late to listen to the news. Nothing. But next day's paper had it. Two more. Gas mains? Explosives lorry? No, I could not wait to be back.

The girls were still chortling with glee when I arrived. One of our CC post team – the one supposed to be having her ten minutes' rest – had been out on the roof and, such is the cussedness of the human spirit, had used her time gazing out to sea. Eastwards. And she saw it. An unmistakeable zigzag trace, going upward from the horizon.

'Big Ben!' she shouted, racing back indoors. 'I mean, Fireworks! Out there – over there – look!'

The launching-pad was not in the Pas-de-Calais. It proved to be on Walcheren Island, in the Netherlands.

The pattern of attacks changed. Whereas the robot-like flying bombs, the V1s, had come over in droves, blaring their way across the sky dozen by dozen, cutting out and taking that stomach-shrinking ten seconds or so before exploding, these things brought no warning. You were dead before you heard anything.

If only we had known what we were trying to locate. If only the RAF bombing crews had known what they were trying to destroy. But if we had known, it would only have caused us to despair. Perhaps it was as well. We gave them two, three, four locations every day. Strangely, the figures never worked out exactly the same. This worried us a bit, because you would expect only one or two launching-places.

Of course, when the rocket attacks went on, in spite of their raids, the RAF blamed us. One or two Visits From On High took place, and we half-heard the old 'inefficient women', 'What can you expect?' etc etc jibes once more.

I was at that time receiving a bombardment of poetically

romantic letters from a certain Martello tower near Clacton, and one day the sender came to see me in St Margaret's. He told me about the efforts being made to engage the V2s by the new coastal batteries. 'Welterweight' these batteries were called, being a mixture of heavy and light, using a variety of ammunition. A ten-second engagement was being planned for. It was impossible to track the thing on its upward flight: too far away or on its level flight which was too fast; but at the end, when it began to fall, it took ten seconds to reach the earth, and that gave time for two rounds to be fired. Whether it was ever successful, I never heard. Whether it was every seriously tried, I do not know.

But the rockets continued to fall, in an uncanny sort of seven-mile curve, on the inner, older suburbs of terraced, freehold, two-storeyed houses, now regarded as old-fashioned, and the gardens too small. They were a fat target for an enemy who now wanted to slaughter populations. There were 'incidents' south of the river, too.

Life in St Margaret's Bay pleased us well. We soon adapted to it. At the end of Granville Road, where we were, was the bus stop, with a twenty-minute service in both directions, to Dover one way and Deal the other. Dover had more attractions, and we went there fairly often. There was no going home for odd days from here, and we had to wait for proper leave. Well, I had had mine, until Christmas. We explored. In the twelve hours between watches, there was time to sleep and have an outing. We discovered a little house with a big garden, in the village of St Margaret's-at-Cliffe, now turned into an open-air café, where the husband grew the lettuces and tomatoes, and the wife made the salad sandwiches.

Every day we tried to make sure that two or three of us got to Canterbury. A truck went in and came back, and they would always take a few of us. The visit to the Survey Regiment's place was priority. It was a big square, panelled room, dark except for the big table. The whole of south-east England and much of the opposite coast lay mapped on it, and a hundred little torches shone upward from the map onto a vertical glass screen which could be slid around above them. Each torch was linked to its big brother, the radio direction finder in the actual place in the real world, in Kent, that the torch represented on the map. And they all shone upward in different directions, making crazy patterns on the screen.

An alert sounded, and all the torches went mad, then settled. The patterns they made were crazier than ever. A phone rang, and a number was received. Eastings and northings. We girls craned over to see. This is what we had come for. The co-ordinates were where a rocket had fallen.

One end of the high glass screen – the London end – was fixed to the point that the phoned number located. North-east London again. No, not near any of our homes this time. We thanked the men and left them to their work. They were doing what we were trying to do: pinpoint the place where the rocket had been fired.

Where we were concerned, for our families' sakes, with the receiving end of the screen, they were interested in the other. If you swing that end round, there comes a magic moment when the little lights all make a smooth curve on the glass. This is your missile's trajectory. And up at that end is where it came from. What ingenuity war brings out in people!

You cannot keep a good Royal Engineer from burrowing. Ever since they discovered they could make holes in the Rock of Gibraltar, they have been at it everywhere. The white cliffs of Dover are irresistible to them. We had been told how far the tunnels and galleries went down, beneath Dover Castle, and we were not too surprised to see them working just along the road, near us.

Soon they left, and there began one of the most unpleasant episodes of the whole war, as far as our girls were concerned. Gunfire began, from Calais. Shelling, that is. It was not heavy; it did not do very much damage, in comparison with the attacks on cities; but its effect was insidious and cumulative. Every quarter of an hour – on the hour, on the quarter, on the half and on the quarter-to – a shell was fired across the Channel. Only one shell, aimed at some point along our bit of coast. Mainly they fell in or near Dover, but the range was wide, and there was no pattern to it. The next one could fall anywhere. Every quarter of an hour, all day and all night. Day after day. Every time the clock chimes, another 'Boom!' You swallow, and breathe again. Not us, this time.

It was ridiculous to be afraid. The chance of being hit was so remote; it bore no relation to Blitz conditions; and yet, after the first week of it – at the end of the second week of it, it got harder to make light of it. It began to be unnerving. And then the inevitable order came. No more wandering up to the village on off-duty times; no going to Canterbury; no bus-riding to Dover. Every off-duty moment that was not actually a meal-time we had to spend in the deep shelters that the REs had made for us.

There were seventy steps down, each nearly a foot deep. It was bad enough climbing up them, but at least you had the incentive of fresh air. It was going down that I found difficult. Boots and ankle-gripping leather gaiters. It was too much for my little legs. I had to jump down every step. At the bottom, there were two tunnels. One for the men, one for us. There was an inter-connecting passage for safety's sake, with a curtain for modesty's sake. Our section must have had sixty or seventy beds packed closely side-by-side, and chemical Elsan loos up at the end, behind curtains. There were forty-four of us kines, then the GD clerks, the orderlies and the cooks.

Goodbye to our sea-view bedroom. Goodbye to drifting off to sleep to the sound of the mournful cry of the buoy, just out to sea. We still spent some time in there, of course, but they insisted that we sleep in the shelter. It was eerie, changing watch in the middle of the night, with no living thing above ground except our small squads and sentries. We did have one 'incident', however.

One of the shells did come perilously near us. It fell near Kine Station 'Love'. Eileen Cheetham – or was it Madge Littler? – felt, and they all heard, something hit her steel helmet. One of the others picked up the bit of shrapnel, and she took off the hat and eagerly searched it for the dent. Disappointingly, there was only the merest scratch. Our only bit of enemy action! While on watch, of course, we still had the air, the sky, the sea and the hope that we were doing something significant. But as the evenings drew in and the rocket attacks went on, there was no achievement that we could claim.

One day Kathleen Lavery and I had to be very brave. The detachment at Shorncliffe was depleted for some reason, and they wanted our help. So Kathleen and I were taken over in the 'tilly' truck, and we had to open up the kine hut. It was near a corner of Shorncliffe Camp, between there and the sea. We had come well equipped, with the usual film in a container, the field telephone, batteries, switch box, stop watch, fire-making materials, provisions and a frying-pan. We undid the padlock and slid back the roof. About a thousand spiders, of all sizes, shapes and colours, filled the place.

It took us nearly five minutes to gather up all our courage. We scrambled up into the camp and begged at the cookhouse door for help. How they laughed at us! We sat down on their doorstep while they cleared the hut, and we tried not to listen to what they had to say. Spiders? Neither of us had that kind of courage.

On 10 November the nation was told for the first time about the V2, and what it was. Churchill himself made a speech and told the country the truth. From then on, individual attacks were reported, but cautiously, rather vague as to detail. It was not until near the end of the month that a full report was allowed to be made, of the hit at New Cross Woolworth's, where over a hundred people were killed and twice as many injured. But by this time we had been stood down. We were thanked officially, told that there must be some factor that had not been reckoned with and that we could now await our postings. So that was that.

To have a trade in the Army gives you certain entitlements. You may have cooks, and orderlies to help those cooks and to do the cleaning of everything except sleeping-quarters. We were not now exercising our trade; therefore, no cooks, no orderlies. So there we were left, in the middle of St Margaret's, kine officers and kine ATS, with no one to feed us. News soon came that we should be posted in a fortnight's time, but in the meantime we must manage.

I do not remember using the shelters at this time. Probably our forces across the Channel had overrun the gun, and the shelling had stopped. The war was moving into its final phase. Only the bombardment of London went on.

We had a fortnight with no duties, except the usual duty auxiliary and fire piquet. We had a larder full of food, and daily arrivals of meat, vegetables and bread. Lois got up a list. We were to write, beside our names, anything at all that we felt we could cook, and also the name of a friend who would help.

I felt rather confident about rice pudding. It could be nice, if plenty of 'densy (condensed) milk and a bit of butter went into it. I had had an encounter with rice pudding while looking after two invalids in my aunt's house at Wycombe, where my father and I had taken Mummy when she was recovering from her operation, and her sister had chosen that moment to have flu. I had learned that you do not put a pound of rice to a pint of milk and was ready to volunteer for something I had mastered.

Some offered sausage-frying, some to make a stew; some optimists volunteered to bake cakes and scones, and some more modestly opted for opening cans of beans and making toast. We all – all forty-four of us – could think of something we could manage. There was only one problem that we had, when the system was in full swing: we were too successful. We had to take energetic walks along the cliff and down the tangled paths, to work up an appetite for the next meal. We had never eaten so well in the Army before.

I enjoyed Gina's friendship. We had a lot of fun. She was creative and artistic, always with some mad idea or other. Once it was plaster casts: we learnt how to make casts of our hands, clenched hands for paper-weights, open hands for ash-trays. Not that she or I smoked, but they looked rather attractive, we thought.

'Ugh!' said some of our ungrateful colleagues. 'They look disgusting.'

We found a victim for another, more ambitious venture. Was it Marion Milnes? I forget, but whoever it was, we persuaded her to let us do a face cast. We arranged drinking-straws up her nose so that she could breathe, and greased her face well and made a very good job of it. Afterwards she called us all sorts of names, but we gave her the mask. It was a beauty. Not a bubble in it. It was Gina who had discovered the figs, back in the summer.

'Do you like figs?'

I had tasted only dried ones, at Christmas times. 'Oh, yes.'

'Here.' Balanced on a leaf were six ambrosial purple figs. Absolutely delicious.

She was wonderful fun to be with. She had a method of fortune-telling that she tried out on me, but all I remember of it was that the four of spades kept turning up – 'Ooh, the marriage card!'. And she knew all the superstitions under the sun. We tried the Hallowe'en thing of looking in the mirror at midnight, with a candle, but no lover looked over my shoulder, nor hers.

She and I pruned and weeded the roses, together with some of the others, and some of them cut the grass. We had found a shop that still sold paints and brushes, and we painted our bedroom walls and woodwork. We invented, on behalf of all kines, the resolve to leave a billet, if it were someone's house, in a better state than we had found it in.

Gina and I lost touch, but I had enjoyed our friendship.

Off, then, we all went again. Verna Holliday, Lois, Kathleen, Flea and Gladys, Joy Dalby and me. We were to go to a place called Great Chart, a small village in Kent, not far from Ashford. Inland. When our little group arrived, the others were already there. You lose some, you gain some. I met Sue Turnpenny, and Verona Loynston-Pickard came back into my life.

There were one or two others, to make up a half-detachment. Jo Booth, who, it turned out, lived in Gidea Park, a mile from where my home was; and Norah Moyes and Ann Hay, who were friends already.

Now the work was different again. Not innovatory gunnery trials, not gunnery practice, not operationally seeking our enemy's lair; this had no end-product that we were told of, and it was all deadly dull routine.

On the other hand, not the discomforts of Manorbierish gales, or Lydsteppish damp, of overcrowded Clacton or the wearisome day-and-night watches at St Margaret's. Here was real comfort in a real English country house, in early Victorian spaciousness. Our Scandinavian cook gloried in her Aga cooker, and we gloried in the great open fireplace and inglenook and the handsome proportions of all the space. It was a great place to spend a winter.

But the work – pages and pages of computations, with no purpose. Not difficult; just boring.

Sue Turnpenny and I began to work as partners. Obviously the great thing is speed, and to check each other's results for errors, so two whose speed is similar work together well. Some pairs could zip along at great speed, needing frequent rests, while some could plod along for hours and hours. Sue and I were good partners, able to work and rest in a sympathetic rhythm, and we could still find something to giggle at when it all got too dreary. Norah Moyes and Ann Hay worked like lightning, with hardly an error, page after page after page.

Catherine Dawson, who had been an unobtrusive presence at St Margaret's, was our officer. She did not seem to be a very happy woman. She grew more silent with us every day. She would come back from mess nights quarrelsome with us in the mornings, arguing petty mathematical details. She tried to get me going one day, trying to make me agree that 18 times 0 was different from 0 times 18. Her hosts of the previous evening must have been ragging her unmercifully. It was all too tiresome. What difference did any of it make?

But against all physical discomforts we were cushioned. From barrack-hut bleakness on one hand, from the growing civilian hardships on the other. Civilian attitudes were changing, as conditions hardened. Everything was shabby, everything dingy.

They tell us now that the British had never been so healthy: that little or no sugar was good for our teeth, that hardly any butter was good for our hearts, that minute quantities of meat are good for the blood pressure and that grey bread was good for just about everything. But none of this did much for the spirits at that time, the coldest winter in living memory.

As for us, we were enjoying the country winter. We enjoyed following the beagles one day across the frozen fields, through scrambly hedges and over stiles; so comfortable was our life that at the first opportunity we went snowballing. We borrowed Linguaphone German from the welfare library, and we growled and hissed and spat at one another in fine style. We had a collection of records: Norah and Ann were Frankie fans; some voted for Bing, and there was Glenn Miller, who delighted everyone: 'Starlight Serenade'; 'Long ago and far away I dreamed a dream one day ...'; 'American Patrol'; 'Spring will be a little late this year ...'; 'I don't know if it's cloudy or bright, Cos I've only got eyes for you, dear ...'. We all took sides for our favourite crooner. You couldn't be loyal to both.

Our relations with Dawson did not improve.

In that isolated place, on the edge of a sleepy village, with no other military establishment anywhere near, it struck us as funny to be paraded out in the front garden early every morning; and one day our usual low instincts left us with only four who could not think of an excuse to dodge it. As it happened, morning inspection consisted of the two tallest, Sue and Verona, and the two shortest, Joy Dalby and me. We tried to arrange ourselves as amusingly as possible, but she continued to look abstracted and did not even listen to the ingenious excuses we made for the absentees. We felt almost remorseful; we felt almost sorry for her. The zest seemed to have gone out of taunting Authority.

A night or two afterwards, our washbasin tap started dripping. Did we send for a plumber? Of course not. A little job like that ... Sue and I got permission to go down to the village to buy a washer. We knew all about changing washers. Were we not kines?

Great Chart was a real old English village. Church, school, pub, general stores; the vicar, the doctor, the teacher, the district nurse; and the Big House. Our house, 'The Limes', was the lodge to the house. We never saw The Family, but Sue knew them vaguely, having been a boarder at Ashford School and known some of the local gentry. She received an invitation to dine there one evening but decided against accepting. She said it was because she had nothing to wear, but she probably didn't trust us to behave ourselves.

The shop sold everything. We were offered two tap washers, of two different sizes. This confused us a bit, but we decided to lash out and bought both. We took all the normal precautions, covering the top of the tap with a dishcloth while taking the top off very gradually, very slowly, and I pressed the rag down while Sue measured and chose the right washer. I dared to release the pressure a bit, and the water offered no resistance. It just dribbled out. We finished in triumph, and our reputation was made. Anything like a fuse or a squeaky hinge came our way to be dealt with. And one day the landing tap dripped. It was inside the maid's broom cupboard: a tap for filling buckets. It had no sink, no drain. It was just dripping onto the polished floor. Immediately above the kitchen. Unfortunately, it was a cold tap, straight from the mains, unlike the one in the bedroom.

While our reputation was still a little tarnished, Sue was sent on a WOSB, and I was nearly due for leave. Then Catherine Dawson was suddenly replaced. Ruby Nicholson was coming to be our CO, and we did not know what to expect. She had been our sergeant at Lydstep, and several of us knew her. It could be ticklish, greeting as officer someone you had known before her elevation. Jessie Wareham was one we had seen recently; she was now a junior commander. She was as inscrutable as ever, her black hair just as straight, her dark eyes just as bright, and for all we could see absolutely unchanged. But we had met Sheila Caws again, and Sheila had been embarrassed to see us. Her old Lydsteppers, whom she had jokingly tucked up in bed in the old Nissen hut, she could not bring herself to address by Christian name, and we felt awkward with her. She did come to see us in Great Chart one day, and things were a little easier, but not much.

Ruby Nicholson turned out to be a different kettle of fish altogether. As garrulous and cheerful as ever, she greeted us all as easily as she ever had as an NCO. She laughed at our Linguaphonic noises, but in an encouraging way, as we sat and sewed pretty underwear and embroidered bottom-drawer table linen. Sue was doing fine crochet work – about a million medallions to join together, and Gladys was having a race with the Soviets shelling Stalingrad, shelling the edge of a petticoat.

The Second Front had begun. The Soviets had taken in Poland on their way to Berlin, which meant that another race was on: who would reach Berlin first – the Soviets or the Western Allies?

Sue came back from her WOSB. Wartime had demanded a shorthand method of selecting officers, and instead of going straight to OCTU, candidates went on a weeding-out forty-eight-hour selection board.

'I don't know what they thought they wanted,' she told us on her return. 'It was something between a Brownie badge and an assault course.' She painted a lovely picture of herself, holding up a half-erected bell-tent single-handed, not hearing, from its stifling folds, the whistle that blew for abandoning the tent, in favour of a net that had to be climbed, about half a mile away. They had to give lecturettes and to drill a specially primed stroppy platoon. Taking the salute on parade; taking drinks with high-ranking officers; but, most sinister of all, the food …

On arrival, they were given asparagus for luncheon, and tough steak. At tea-time, slithery sandwiches, squashy cream cakes and brandy snaps. For breakfast they were served sloppy eggs on over-cooked brittle toast, with the polished table sneering at them; and the heavy fork and narrow knife did not help. The banquet that night was meagre in quantities of food, but generous in cutlery. There was soup, with slimy bits trailing about in it; a quarter of a kipper; chicken on the bone, under-done and obstinate, with green peas and plenty of thin gravy and little hard potatoes; chocolate mousse, cheese with flaky cream crackers and a fresh apple. All this, with a large and impregnable bread roll to go with it.

Sue said she had looked at the chocolate mousse, wondering what hazard was hiding in that. She decided that you were not supposed to eat it all in one mouthful. She didn't, but she was sorely tempted.

I went on leave.

My dad said, 'It's about time this country had a Labour government. It needs to be ruled by idealists, for a change, not by people with beautiful manners whose only real talent is how to make money for themselves.'

I could not bring myself to think about the future just yet. Get all this over first, and then I would think.

There was nothing that I could do, that I wanted to do. Not yet. I wasn't going to make any plans.

12 'Hitler – *Kaput'*

The Netherlands, April and May 1945

Easter was lovely. Binkie, the young goat, had grown up at last and had given birth to two white kids, both nannies. So sweet, so saucy, so full of fun. They had at least one reason to be happy: they were having all their mother's milk. And they were welcome to it. It was all that everyone says about goat's milk, and worse. So different from Bessie's. To be in the same room with a saucerful of it was a punishment, let alone try to drink it. Even the cat would not touch it. But Bessie the Toggenburg was still giving sweet, delicious milk. What a mercy that it had been good, all that time ago.

The plum and damson trees were in bloom, the pear was just beginning, and the cherries and apples were forming their rosettes. Everything felt very normal. Was this the last spring of the war? Could it be? The blackout had been lifted. This was only sensible, for rockets have no eyes. Four or five of them were still falling somewhere in London and its surroundings, every day. If only we kine girls could have stopped them. It was a nightmare of frustration.

Why was I always on leave when anything important happened? A telegram arrived from Ashford, asking me to telephone. Ruby said, 'Now, Doffy, I want you to be calm. Don't get excited, and don't say anything you shouldn't. We've had an invitation. The regiment has invited us to join them. It should be a very interesting party, wouldn't you say so?'

I said, 'But ... they're ...'

It was impossible to utter, on a public telephone line,

the fact that the 11th Survey Regiment were in Belgium, or the Netherlands, or somewhere.

'That's right,' she said. 'Now, will you come? It's entirely a free choice.'

'Oh, yes! Yes!'

'You'd better come back tomorrow morning, then. We're off, first thing next day.'

It was all hustle and bustle and pack-what-you-could. We were to fly from Croydon, which was the major London airport then; and up in the early dawning, into a truck and off. The driver lost himself in the damaged streets and signpost-less suburbs. We watched an aircraft take off at exactly eight o'clock, our flight time, and jokingly said, 'There it goes!' – not dreaming that Our Plane would not wait for us.

Ruby found a flight to Brussels later in the morning, with five empty places, another in the afternoon with nine. So she had to split us. Lois, Sue, Verna, Kathleen and I went first, with strict instructions not to get lost in Brussels before she arrived with the others.

We all went through the 'sausage machine' before we left: document perusal, luggage search, mini-medical inspection, TT and TAB jabs and smallpox scratch, change your money, briefing notes for Belgium and the Netherlands and off you go. It all took less than half-an-hour. If only modern travel were so efficient!

Brussels was not quite what we had expected. Where were the signs of war? Where were the tired, sad faces? The heaps of rubble? 'Poor little Belgium': where was it?

We had not seen anything like Brussels for years. The women in their fine stockings and high-heeled shoes, the perfumed men; the shops groaning with food; cafés with windows full of butter-cream cakes; wines and spirits displayed in shameless profusion, and the aroma of good coffee. Shops there were, full of silk-lace undies, all on sale with no restriction. We could – anyone could – buy as much of all this as we liked.

It is remarkable how quickly disapproval succumbs to temptation. By the time we had taken every possible advantage and were penniless, it was time to meet the others. Piling into the truck with them, we felt slightly ashamed and were pleased when we stopped at Antwerp, where they were able to have a small shopping spree.

We passed rapidly out of Belgium, into the wartime Netherlands. A very different picture.

Verona said, 'I didn't remember to spend all my ha'pennies!'

We had loaded ourselves with small coins, so that we could play pontoon on the deck of the troopship that we were sure would carry us across the Channel – but, of course, the stripped-out Dakota had no room, and the flight gave us no time for deck gambling.

And now we were entering a Theatre of War. Not Behind the Lines, of course: they would never have allowed that to happen to us. We were not the Odettes, the heroines, the immortals. But it was thrill enough. On our sleeves we had sewn the red, white and blue shoulder-flash of the Two One Army Group. It had put the British nose out of joint at first, making Eisenhower the Supreme Commander, with Monty as his subordinate, and the American Second Army over the British First, but we weren't grumbling today.

De Poort Van Kleef was a small hotel, next door to the *Rat Huis*, the town hall, in Breda's main square. All was quiet when we arrived, and there was a smell that we did not want to ask too closely about.

The *chef* greeted us, introduced his girl assistant and told us that dinner would be in half-an-hour, and we went upstairs. The building was narrow to the street but long and spacious, with a bar (unstocked) on the ground floor. The middle floor was a ballroom, and the bedrooms were at the top. Three or four bedrooms on each side of a long corridor, and no windows in the rooms: just skylights. But comfortable. Real beds, not Army ones. Cot-type, like the German variety, and instead of Army blankets, pretty pink and white Jacquard-patterned ones, thick, soft and luxurious. Sue and I decided that that was the type we should put in our bottom drawers, when we came to fill them. The room was small, but just enough room for the two beds, with a table in between.

Dinner was a banquet. The cook, who lived in the town,

had not seen such food, so much food, for years. Things had improved wonderfully for the Dutch since the very recent liberation, but he still could not believe his good fortune. And what he managed to do with Army rations was a revelation.

This was all very well, but what were we doing here? It was, of course, a V2 watch. We hoped, against our better nature, that the rockets were not entirely finished and that we should see them at this, much closer range. By this time, after all that had happened, we wanted to whack the enemy, not have him slide away from us. To have failed on our Kent watching still stung.

There is a place 20 kilometres west of Breda, on the River Maas, called Steenbergen. That was where we were going to spend our nights. The job was a night-time watch. Steenbergen was up nearer the enemy; it was only this southern strip of the Netherlands that had as yet been liberated by the Allies. North of the Maas, and east of the Rhine, the enemy was still well established. The road that leads eastwards from Breda to Tilburg, and then forks to either Eindhoven or 's Hertogenbosch were free, but there was still fighting between there and Nijmegen, in the area between the Maas and the Rhine, and the Canadians were now advancing beyond. We were not far from the front then, and at night only the river would separate us from enemy territory. How exciting! Now, this was something like it!

Ruby said, 'There are twelve of you. You will be divided into two squads of six each, taking alternate nights. But I have arranged that one of the six is always on leave, so the squads will actually be five strong, on any given night. I shall be up there most nights, for part of the time at least.'

It was a simple watching duty without the kines. There was a tiffy truck up there on the site, and they had all our equipment and instruments on board, but not unpacked; perhaps we should need them later, perhaps not. The 'site' proved to be a rubbish dump by the side of the river, which smelt cold and stale, more like a canal smell than a river. On the bank to our left was a sugarbeet factory, and anyone who has ever smelt one of those will appreciate the quality of our environment.

When we settled to a night's watching, two to a sentry box, seated side by side with a rug over our knees, having been told to keep quiet and not show any lights, the air was quiet, and only the water lapping and the occasional burst of laughter from the truck could be heard. Faint rustlings there were, close to; and, as always, our fears were out of proportion. More terrible than the prospect of a squad of German soldiers coming up out of the river, far more frightening than a bomb that might fall, was the thought of the rats that infested the dump where we were. It was commonplace to have one run over your feet. Happily we were well protected and wrapped up, but it was not a very pleasant sensation.

Every other night we went on watch; and Ruby made a leave roster. Every day, two of us could be spared. That meant that we could have a jaunt somewhere every six days. Some of us could speak German and could therefore understand Dutch when it was spoken, so Ruby's list was very interesting. She distributed the German-speakers such that on every other of your days off one of you could speak German, and on the alternate day one of you at least could speak French. So it could be Tilburg or Eindhoven or Nijmegen or Bergen-op-Zoom on one day, and six days later Brussels or Mechlin or Antwerp.

The town mayor was very kind to us: we drew our pay in gulden, but if we had a leave pass to Belgium, he would change it into francs. There was so little that could be bought in the Netherlands: there were a few books left in the secondhand-book shop, there were a few postcards of the town, but not much else. We all had a pair of wooden shoes made to measure, and I had a pair to take home for my father. It was a fascinating experience, watching the *clompen* being shaped, and they looked much bigger close-to than in the pictures we had seen. They are incredibly uncomfortable to wear. The instep has to take the weight – bonk – at each step, and it feels like being flogged across the feet. But there was so little to buy, and we would have liked to spend our money there, if we could.

Now we saw the difference between our own beleaguered island, bombed and harassed, and a country where the enemy had actually set his foot. What we saw made us humble. Compared to this, we in Britain did not know what war was. It was not just the dearth of material goods and food, not just the empty shops, the poor clothes, the fear of danger: there was that in people's eyes here that we had never seen before. They were so grateful for their liberation, so pathetic. A proud little nation, a trading people, and they had been through experiences that makes everyone into a beggar. They would not be that but could not help exclaiming at the quality of our leather shoes, and we resolved to do our old soldier's trick of buying new ones from our stores, pretending we had lost them. They would not ask for tobacco or sweets, but they had nothing left to trade with.

Small boys would follow us about in the street or run after the truck we were riding in: 'Souvenir for Mama? Cigarette for Papa? Chocolate for me?' Giggle, giggle. We could not resist them, although we knew the young monkeys would smoke the cigarettes themselves.

Ordinary people in the street shunned us at first, in Breda, mistaking us for Dutch Army girls, who were not popular. But as soon as they knew we were British, they glowed and welcomed us with what hospitality they could offer. Several families we met in Breda and in Bergen-op-Zoom, where some of our survey men were billeted. Tea would be offered – without milk or sugar, of course: there was none. The pot of tea was put in a kind of nest cosy and topped up with boiling water as the evening proceeded. The cup of tea, always served in the best china, was accompanied by a square of chocolate that some soldier had given to one of the family. There was plenty of Hollands gin, but the only thinner they had was blackcurrant purée, like the stuff the British Min. of Food issued for babies. But it is possible to have quite a party on these modest refreshments, all talking in our own languages and understanding one another wonderfully.

A dance was organized for us at Bergen, one day, and we could see that the festive air had been awaited for a long time. It was so recent, their freedom from the Germans, not much more than a few days. They would not be called 'Dutch': it sounded too much like '*Deutsch*'. We had to say

'Hollandsch', or *'Nederlandsch'*.

The second time we went to a dance there, we met again a group of Free French soldiers. During the evening they received a message and disappeared. The whisper went round that they had been called to the front line, which was not so many miles away and where a particularly unpopular German unit was fighting. The word 'Oradour' was heard. 'They don't take prisoners. They are very hard men. They come from a village – Oradour – where the Germans slaughtered all they could find, while these young men were away, fighting for France.'

A young girl came into the hall, with a boy too young to be a lover. The barman moved down to the other end, and we realized that every back was turned towards them. One of our new friends whispered, *'Deutsche Wrouw.'* The girl wasn't really German, of course, but she had been one of the hated collaborators. She looked plump and well-fed, with pretty clothes and good make-up, but she had a head-scarf tied tight about her neck and face. We had heard that in France girls who had fraternized with the Germans had had their heads shaved. Was this –? The music went on; we danced another dance. It was grotesque.

The public services in the region were pitiful: there was mains water, if you were prepared to be patient; the drains smelt very bad in some parts of the town, and the canals stank. The liberating armies were doing what they could, but they were too busy fighting to spare many men for engineering work. They had made petrol available where they could, and there was paraffin oil for anyone who could make use of it. But the town gas supply no one could do much about. It was strictly rationed. Fifteen minutes just before eight in the morning, for breakfast; half an hour at noon, and another quarter at five o'clock. And that was all. The only water heating for washing in our hotel was from an old geyser in the bathroom on our floor, and we developed a method whereby the one who was in the bath let everyone else come and fill a jug, while the gas still flowed. Three four, or more, can bath in half-an-hour, and there is still time for everyone else to be served. Unhappily I was last bather on one occasion, and the water ran cold while there were yet only two warm inches in the bath, so I hastily turned the control. It responded immediately, and a douche of cold water descended on me from a large and unsuspected shower head. Aargh!

Verona and Jo and Sue and Kathleen and I set out our pontoon on the big table just inside the plate-glass window one day, and all the ha'pennies that had been brought with us. Just as we began to play, a man who was passing glanced in at us and asked to come in.

'You play cards for money?' he enquired.

'Oh, yes,' we said. 'Come and join us.'

He was good-looking and well dressed and spoke very good English. This, naturally, made us suspicious of him. But we let him join in the game, and when he realized the scale of our gambling and the value of the stakes, he laughed and entered into the spirit of the thing very good-naturedly. It seemed that he ran the local newspaper, which had not been published since the German occupation had begun; now he could not begin publishing again, for want of newsprint.

'Paper is almost unobtainable in Nederland. If only I had Belgian francs: anything can be bought in Belgium.'

In a company of young girls, it is always the vicar's daughter who is brave enough to say what is in everyone else's mind.

'What exchange rate would you give us,' Verona asked him, 'if we could get you some francs?'

He offered us a quite generous profit, and we did a deal with him, there and then, and a promise of more, after pay-day. It must have been during our third week there that we met him, and Verona was the only one of us that had not spent most of her money, so she did rather well.

The nightly watch went on, but no smoke trails appeared for us. It looked as though we had come on a fools' errand, after all. But it removed a great weight off the hearts of some of us.

Being, as we were, such a small unit, some already friends, we found it easy to get know one another. We talked on every subject under the sun. Names, Christian names, came under discussion one day. It was interesting, having a Verona and a Verna in the same small group.

'If Florence Nightingale's father could call his daughter after his favourite city, my dad thought he'd do the same thing.'

As for Verna, her father (is it always fathers who name daughters?) had two favourite names: Flora, the fair Flora, and Verna.

'If it is a girl and she is fair, let's call her Flora Verna; and if she's dark, Verna Flora.'

Verna, who is still a great giggler, had us laughing too when she told us how she had stayed fair just long enough to be christened; then, to confound everyone, her eyes and hair turned dark.

Every one of our names had some story behind it, but our histories were not all comic. Verna had joined up in the summer of 1942, was on the same course as Flea Pringle and Gladys Fenton and had been posted to the practice camp at Bude, where she had met Jo Booth and Mary Wilkin, Jo's friend. She had met, almost immediately, a young aircraftman whose duty was to pay out the steel towing cable with the target drogue, from the plane, during practice firing. He and Verna were married; and only a few weeks afterwards, he was killed. The cable wrapped itself round him, and he was dead almost immediately. We were not all without sorrows.

Then, of course, it was, 'How did you come to join up?' and 'What are you doing in the Army anyway?'

Jo, who had no aspirations beyond the single stripe she wore, in spite of her qualifications, said she had come in for a quiet life. Another teacher! She was a couple of years older than Sue and me and had already been teaching for two years when the war started. It was a 'good' school for girls: a boarding school, with a very proper reputation. She, being the lively, witty and independent girl that she was, probably did not fit in very well with the rest of such a school staff, being neither jolly-hockey-sticks (though she did play the game, and well) nor drily scholarly. She had had a little old Austin 7, or something of the sort, and her idea of an evening out was a few miles' drive and an hour or two in some country pub, where she would taste the ale and listen to the old countrymen's tales. Eventually, inevitably, it was Noticed. A Member of this

Staff had been seen entering a Public House, and Jo was asked very politely to resign, at her earliest convenience. So she had joined up, into kines.

Breda was worth exploring. Flea and I found Dutch William, standing at the head of the canal, near the public library. Our Williamanmary King William, who had brought back strictness to us naturally puritanical British. Wee Willie Winkie. There he stood, looking very handsome. The Dutch, we discovered, are very proud of him. Another thing that struck Flea and me about the Netherlands was the light, that pale golden light that is in all the old Dutch paintings, that sharpens edges and flatters brick; it is there, to be seen. Not even East Anglia has such light.

We went into the public library for something, and they were very charming to us and offered to lend us anything we wanted.

Sue and I went to the market. Countrywomen were there, with what little they could spare to sell, with their lace caps and gold 'horns' which represented their dowries, we were told. I bought a dozen tulips and found only ten in my dozen. Of course – we were on the Continent.

In spite of the fact that we were only the river's width from the enemy and not far from the constantly shifting front line, we only once had a sniff of the German Army, ourselves. We kine girls, we five-at-a-time little band, we did see the Enemy once – or, rather, heard him.

It was in the middle of the night, when watching becomes hard work. Nothing was happening. Scanning the ever-empty sky, empty save for the stars, we had only the occasional rustling among the rubbish at our feet to keep us wide awake. The occupants of the tiffy truck were quiet; the skyline was only an imagined denser black than the rest of the dark, and the regular sound of lapping water was hypnotic. We had settled after a change-over, and just when the waiting for the dawn seemed unbearable, a breath of air passed over the water, the rat scuttling ceased and the sound of creaking wood interrupted the river's rhythm.

Then, footsteps in the dark; a shaft of light from the factory appeared and vanished. Hands laid hold of us: 'Come on – don't hang about. Into the truck – quick!' And ignominiously we were bundled into our tiffy truck and locked in.

This was the nearest we ever came to contact with the foe, who turned out to be a rowing-boat load of German soldiers, coming across from the Netherlands they were still occupying, north of the river, to the sugarbeet factory, to do a black-market deal of food for cigarettes. But they were genuine enemy troops, armed, and we had nearly seen them.

We made a great deal of fuss, afterwards, about having been thus locked up, as soon as anything exciting happened, but our mock-indignation cut no ice with our protectors – or, to tell the truth, with ourselves. For four years we had felt like soldiers, 'doing a man's job', sharing the discomforts of military life, subduing ourselves to the discipline of the service; but this last barrier which no one ever discussed, of course, we should never breach. Dress us in khaki, make us march up and down, stripe us and pip us into artificial ranks, but soldiers we were not, and never could be. In many ways those weeks we spent on the edge of the war zone changed our feelings and changed us.

The next day, there were two pieces of news. First, the V2 site had been captured by our troops, and we would not be required to go on duty that night, until further notice.

The second was that the queen was coming to Breda. Queen Wilhelmina, accompanied by Princess Juliana, was coming to welcome the town back to freedom and to show herself to her people after her long exile. She had spent the war in Britain, refusing to cross the Atlantic but insisting that Juliana and the children go to Canada. Now they had returned to their country. A protocol was invented for these town visits: the queen sent a message to the mayor that she would like to hear the children sing, and the occasion took the form of a concert, with all the children formed up in the town square, and the queen and the princess on the step of the town hall, accompanied by the town's dignitaries. It was simple. It required no complicated parades or banquets, and it allowed everyone to see the royal party.

And we were living next door! Of course, we begged to be allowed to go down and join the crowds, but there were strict instructions that the only non-Breda people allowed into the square were the press. What genius among us decided that the possession of a camera could lend verisimilitude to our deceit, I forget; but, as we said, if one of us got a good shot, we might sell it to the Card Sharp, who might put it into his paper. So those of us with a camera were allowed into the street. The children were all assembled, and it was cold, waiting for the royal party. My hands were cold, and I called up to the girls leaning out of the upstairs windows to throw me down a pair of gloves. The noise in the square was increasing; the band struck up, and my mime of cold was misunderstood; someone fetched a greatcoat from our bedroom and threw that down. I had it on just as the royal limousine arrived, and just buttoned it up in time. I thought that the queen gave me a special smile. It was Sue's coat I had on. But we took our pictures and got a few quite recognizable snaps of the queen in her fur-trimmed coat and large hat, and of Juliana in her very chic white toque.

Then, in that sweet and sudden spring, after so cold a winter – then, what a wonderful moment it was to meet the man of my dreams: a tall, handsome, if not dark stranger. It was fun, having someone calling each evening, to see if he could take me out, having rides in a jeep, to be given a birthday bottle of champagne and to be taken to the circus. A crowd of us went that night, to – oh! the Continental circus! The adagio dancers, apparently naked under the pink lights; the contortionist, running about like a horrible spider. The clowns! They frightened me, at first sight, at the thought of what they might do next. And the noise! The terrible sound of release laughter; on one hand the heavy ho-ho-ho of the locals, and then the guffaws and sudden belly-laughs that only soldiers can make.

My Canadian paratrooper was still suffering from the shock of a monstrous experience that his unit had had forced upon them very recently. They had come upon one of the concentration camps that everyone had heard of and that nobody could believe in. It must be, reasonable people said, our Ministry of Information, playing a trick learned from the enemy, the propaganda trick to raise our hatred more energetically for the *coup-de-grâce*.

The evidence was there; but evidence, said popular opinion, could be falsified. There were even photographs; but photographs, we said, could be faked. Refugees had managed to escape and told their dreadful tales, and fair-minded folk thought that they were the imaginings of the distraught. But he had seen, and he trembled as he laughed.

And the clowns whipped up their audience's old terrors into gales of laughter, with bombs filled with flour, guns firing water, and fireworks which fizzled. They mocked rape, and the girls who did not wait to be raped; they approached both these scenes with scissors so realistic that you didn't know where to look; they mocked starvation with skeletons pursuing great sausages which turned out to be balloons, and all their attempts at violence ended in tripping up, collisions, falling from great heights and being run over by their trick truck; and between the bare-back riding and the acrobats they did more wicked and lewd and suggestive things with gallons and gallons of water than could be imagined or endured. And we, carefully brought up and carefully protected British girls, who had never been raped, never been threatened with torture, nor seen our parents killed before our eyes, gave in at last and laughed till we cried. But we did not understand, on that day so long ago, the healing power of those vile, coarse, face-painted Merry-Andrews that was more effective than a hundred doctors.

It was stronger stuff than could ever be allowed into Britain.

The time went quickly enough. Most of us managed to visit Antwerp as well as Brussels, where the Army had bagged one of the biggest hotels to become a NAAFI club, in which a bed could be had for a shilling or so. It gave us great pleasure to sweep up the marble staircase, round the colonnaded balcony, to buy a penny cup of NAAFI tea.

Even here it tasted just the same.

Flea and I went shopping in Malines/Mechlin to buy lace for presents; and one day Jo and I were all dressed and ready to go to Nijmegen with a twenty-four-hour pass, hoping to stay the night there and perhaps have the thrill of crossing the Rhine, when the eight o'clock radio news mentioned the fact that our advance had been halted and that the Canadians had fallen back to Nijmegen. So we decided not to go. But a few days later we did spend an hour or two there and were shocked to see the lines of tanks parked at the side of the road, with the letters US painted on them in crude whitewash. It took us a minute or two to work out what the letters meant: not the United States, but Unserviceable. There were dozens of them.

The saddest thing of all that happened while we were in Breda was the death of Franklin D. Roosevelt. We had been there only about a week when it happened. It was almost the first thing we heard on the radio that had been rigged up for us. It must, we thought, be so near the end of the war – the war in Europe, that is; and all British people at that time, I think, regretted that he did not live to see what he had worked so hard to achieve.

On Wednesday 2 May Flea, Norah and I came back from another day in Brussels, to hear that we had all been posted home. On Saturday at 6.30 in the morning we were to leave. There were mixed feelings on our part about this. Since we had heard officially that the V2 sites near the Hague had been overrun, there was not much point in our staying; we had done a fair amount of sightseeing; our Army friends and beaux had left; and things, though pleasant, were a bit slack. So we accepted the situation. After all, there was little we could do about it. So on Friday night we got ourselves packed ready for the morning and went to the dance at Bergen.

'Don't forget,' Ruby told us, 'I want you back for a good night's sleep, and out on this pavement at six o'clock sharp, with all your kit. The truck is coming at 6.30, and we're catching the boat at Ostend. Don't make your beds when you get up: leave the blankets folded and the laundry in the corridor. And we're not going to miss this boat.

So off we went. When the dancing had been going on for about an hour, the band suddenly stopped playing. The kitchen door was open, and a woman was seated at the telephone, straining to hear what was being said and gesturing with her free hand, imploring silence from all of us in the hall. She was laughing and crying, yelling and screaming, then listening again. The Dutch people around us went mad, and we could now make out something of what the woman on the phone was saying.

'Hitler – *kaput!*' she kept repeating. '*Kaput* – Hitler – *kaput* – *Duitsland* – *kaput*! Feeneesh – all feeneesh!'

People burst into tears; there were a few minutes of hugs and kisses, riotous fandangos and handing more drinks round, before the dance was declared abandoned and we girls were rounded up and driven back to Breda.

The town was blazing, alight and mad. Shutters had been torn down from windows and were burning in great bonfires at all the street corners. The windows had been flung open, and all the lights were on. Two hours before this we had left a town completely blacked out, a wartime town near a fighting front, and we came back to delirium. The streets were already filled with dancing crowds, singing as they went; and here we were, in the middle of it. It never occurred to us to go into the hotel. Who would drag us away from this glorious moment? And who could go indoors on such a night?

By twos and threes we were caught up in the dancing, joining on the lines stretched across the streets, arm-in-arm, dancing along past windows where older people leaned out and beckoned some to come in. It was too noisy to hear what anyone said, but at some point the man who was hauling me along realized that I was British, and Sue as well, and he gave a great bellow, gathered a crowd from the dancing mass and bore us all off to his parents' house, where we were entertained royally, with the bottles they had kept for just this night.

After a little while, off we went again and joined the exultant crowds. By this time the bonfires were beginning to burn low, and out of the houses furniture was being brought: chairs, tables, sofas, to keep the fires alight. One man we saw struggling along with a door in his arms. And all this time the capering went on. Along the street, round the corner, across the square, down another street, along by the canal, up another street, where yet another round-up of us British girls took place, and another party. We must have been in about a dozen houses that night. And in every one we were invited to go with them, as soon as they could find transport, across the River Maas, to where their relatives were, and to help them find brothers, sisters, cousins and, in some cases, their old parents, whom they had not heard from for years.

We accepted all the invitations, feeling sure that our posting would have to be postponed. It was out of the question that we should leave now, at this moment. During that night we also encountered some of our own chaps, who were planning the Victory Parade into Brussels the next day: would we come?

Oh, yes!

The sky began to lighten, the fires had burned away, leaving only a few bedsprings among the red ashes. The crowds had melted away, and some of the windows were closing.

Sue and I, Verona and Verna decided to go and find the others. When we arrived at De Poort van Kleef, Ruby was standing on the pavement, and Joy, Ann, Norah and Kathleen were just coming round the other corner. Ruby was cross.

'Wherever have you been?' she demanded. 'It's after six, the transport's coming at half-past, and – look at you! Whatever do you look like? I was going to allow you to travel in battledress, but you'll have to go like that, now. Go upstairs and tidy yourselves up a bit. And strip those beds off. You can't expect Elsa to do all that for you.'

We did feel a bit ashamed, and we tidied up hastily, like naughty children. Poor Lois looked really embarrassed. She had been duty dog the night before and had had to stay with Ruby, who had been getting more and more fretty all night. Jo was with them too. Jo did not go to dances.

But what about our Victory Parade? And going up into the other part of the Netherlands?

Ruby forgave us after a little while, and she told us what

the BBC broadcast had said. All German forces had surrendered in the Netherlands and Denmark and part of Germany, and mopping-up operations were going on, right across towards Berlin. Hitler had committed suicide. Victory Day would be announced as soon as possible.

As for us, we slept for most of the Channel crossing, still bemused by the suddenness of last night's events.

And as we joggled along on our way to Canterbury in the three-ton Scammel truck, how could we know that we should make closer acquaintance with the V2 rocket, later on in the year, to touch and feel and know its secrets and to be part of a military operation that would begin to change our attitude towards the hated adversary and take from our hearts some of its horrors, to enlarge our perception of the size of the world we live in, extending our aspirations out into space?

But at this moment, all we felt was excitement that the Western part of the war was over, and deepening thankfulness; and we allowed ourselves to forget for a few hours that the whole of the Far East was still in bitter conflict, and that more and harder things remained to be done.

This was our moment. Our cities were safe; our parents could begin to live again. No enemy had come to violate our land and leave the stains and stench of battle. How sweet England smelt! We had never noticed it before.

And it was the beginning of May.

Glossary

The three forces, RN, Army and RAF, have a bad habit of speaking almost entirely in initials. They are worse than the Civil Service. Sometimes the complication of the Royal Signals alphabet creeps in. We all know checkpoint Charlie: this is merely Signalspeak for the third checkpoint in a series. This (spoken) alphabet was invented to improve clarity on the field telephones used in noisy surroundings.

The first one, used during the First World War, began: Ack, Beer, Charlie, Don … Later it was improved to: Able, Baker, Charlie, Dog …

The Army, being conservative, still calls a dispatch rider a 'Don R' as well as saying 'Ack Ack' for anti-aircraft.

AA (pronounced ay ay): Automobile Association.

AA (pronounced ack ack): anti-aircraft.

AIG (Ack I G): Assistant instructor of gunnery. A battery sergeant-major, distinguished as an instructor by the white band round his cap.

ATS: Auxiliary Territorial Service, founded in 1938, in succession to Queen Mary's Army Auxiliary Service of the First World War.

BSM (RA): Battery sergeant-major

CSM (infantry): Company sergeant-major. Equivalent rank to BSM.

Barrack night: Once a week everyone stayed in quarters all evening, for mending and smartening up kit.

CIG: Chief instructor of gunnery. Usually a colonel. The commanding officer of a school of gunnery or a practice camp.

ENSA (pronounced 'ensa'): Entertainments National Services Association.

GD: General duties, performed by those without a trade. They were the orderlies, who performed all the unskilled jobs in a camp.
Those who were in technical trades – ack-ack instrument operators, drivers, K/T operators and radar operators – tended to lump all clerical, cookhouse and stores people together as 'GD'. And we 'kines', the KT operators, applied this term, incorrectly and off-handedly, to administration officers.

Field telephone: a handset, linked by a single wire to its mate, the electrical circuit being completed by earthing. It was a handy device, but suffered a lot of interference. The call-signal was a hand-operated buzzer.

Duty officer (officer-of-the-day), **Duty auxiliary, Duty NCO**: Everyone took turns at this unpopular duty: officers to take inspections, hear complaints, sort out daily problems with the day's NCO; and the duty auxiliary, or private, to run errands or take messages, etc.

IG: Instructor of gunnery. Usually a senior officer, a major, distinguished by a red band round his cap.

HAA: (pronounced 'heavy ack-ack'): Heavy anti-aircraft. Usually any AA unit whose guns have a bore of 3.7 inches or more.

LAA (pronounced 'light ack-ack'): Guns with a smaller bore, usually more easily mobile than the 'heavies'.

NAAFI: Navy, Army and Air Force Institutes. This organization provides (licensed) canteens and/or shops in all military camps and residential clubs on overseas stations.

OCTU: Officer Cadets Training Unit.

WAAF: Women's Auxiliary Air Force.

WOSB (pronounced 'wosbee'): War Office Selection Board, a 48-hour preliminary to the full officer training at OCTU.

WO: Warrant officer. Any non-commissioned rank above sergeant (sergeant-majors).

WRNS: Women's Royal Naval Service

WRAC: Women's Royal Army Corps.

When women were given equal status with the army, and the royal warrant was bestowed, there was a problem with the new name. *Royal* Auxiliary Territorial Service? But nobody wanted to be called 'Rats'. So a completely different name was adopted (WRAC). The new name, status and uniform date from 1949.

Index